WOMEN'S MOVEMENT IN: KUWAIT, EGYPT, IRAN AND THE UK

Amani Saleh Alessa

authorHOUSE®

AuthorHouse™ UK Ltd.
500 Avebury Boulevard
Central Milton Keynes, MK9 2BE
www.authorhouse.co.uk
Phone: 08001974150

First published by AuthorHouse 1/7/2010

ISBN: 978-1-4490-3164-0 (e)
ISBN: 978-1-4490-3163-3 (sc)
ISBN: 978-1-4490-3162-6 (hc)

Library of Congress Control Number: 2009914341

This book is printed on acid-free paper.

I. INTRODUCTION

As the sociologist Mohammad Al-Rumaihi has discussed, any one
society within the Arabic peninsula is not very different from any
other, especially if the issue under examination concerns women.[1]
Al-Rumaihi stated that parts of Arabic society can be described as
a 'backward society' in economic, cultural and social terms. He
described how attitudes towards women are also included in this
definition. The main problem of women in Arabic society is the
ignorance of their humanity; even women themselves are unaware

---

[1] Mohammad Al-Rumaihi. Athar Alnaft ala Wathe' Almara' Alarabia fe
Alkhaleej. In: Al-Mara' wa Douroha fe Harakat Al-Wehda Al-Arabia (Women's
Role in Arab Unity). Ali Shalaq 'et.al'. (Lebanon: Markaz Derasat Al-Wehda
Al-Arabia, 1993) pp 231-251.

of this. In spite of the statistics regarding women as educators and workers, it does not help to change the 'backward' view towards women. Also, according to Al-Rumaihi, there are no temptations to awaken women and, if there were any, they would only be artificial ones. In this book, three women's movements in three Middle East countries -- Kuwait, Egypt, and Iran -- will be discussed. The Middle East countries generally share some similarities such as religion, tradition, and occupation experiences.

Although Kuwait only has a short history of the women's movement it nevertheless shares some similarities with the women's movement in Egypt and Iran. The fact that Egypt is part of the Arabic nation, and has a long history of struggles against colonialism in which women played a major part, is an effective factor on Kuwaitis in general. Also, as Egypt used to have a dominant role in the region, its experiences, including the women's movement, were inspiring. Huda Sha'rawi's[2] demeanour quickly spread throughout the Arab countries, and was also taught in schools. On the other hand, both the location of Iran as a neighbour of Kuwaitis position and as representative of the major Muslim denomination 'Shia', was also influential on Kuwaitis since about 15 to 25% of Kuwaitis are Shia (in 1980s).[3] Moreover, as Iran is an Islamic country, all its acts and laws are based on Islam. The three countries share nearly the same degrading attitude towards women and, to a certain extent,

---

[2]   A famous activist in Egypt.

[3]   The Library of Congress. *Kuwait- Society.* [online] [undated] available from: http://www.country-data.com/cgi-bin/query/r-7583.html
[Accessed 11th June. 2009]

they experienced many of the same incidents such as colonism, war, and liberation although in different time periods.

A discussion of each country will begin with highlighting how the women's movement was initiated and will take into consideration the surrounding environment; the campaign for women's rights; the women's role in the political history; and the achievements that women have gained.

The similarities in Middle Eastern societies' points of view towards women and the fight that accompanied the campaign for women's rights will then be compared with the women's movement in a Western country, the UK. The study of the women's movement in the UK is important because it represents a different culture from the Middle Eastern one. However, women in the UK had also suffered from the deprivation of many rights for a long time. They organised many different campaigns before they were able to gain a certain level of equality to men. The most controversial issue in the women's movement in each of these four countries is the participation of men. Unlike in the Middle East countries, in the UK men had also participated in women's rights campaigns by organising societies; this strongly reflects the different attitude towards women between the four countries.

Finally, in each country, there was a major event that affected women directly. In Kuwait, it was the oil discovery while in Egypt was the 1952 Revolution. Although Iran passed through many different revolutions the 1925, and 1979 Revolutions had the most effect on women's rights. In the UK the First World War was an inspiring event for women's rights legislation.

2. The Women's Movement in Kuwait

Before the discovery of oil, life in Kuwait was very different to what it is now. People were divided into two groups: the Bedouins and the city dwellers. The Bedouins lived in the deserts. The main profession of the city dwellers was 'pearling'.[4] This job required

---

[4]   Men earned their livelihood by going deep sea fishing for pearls several months of the year.

for the men to leave home for about 3 months each year. During that time, women took care of the house.[5]

The Kuwaiti society — as in any Middle Eastern one — is formed upon the absolute power of the father or the eldest male. This patriarchal system assured women's subordination. The father, who in many cases has more than one wife, used to make all of the decisions in all of the family matters. He would even decide on his sons' behalf to whom they would marry. Deciding for the daughters is a given fact.[6]

The architecture during that time supported the idea of women as a lower class gender. Houses did not have any windows, so that women could neither be heard nor seen, or see any strangers. Also, men and women had separate guest rooms. In some families, women and men would not sit together to have a meal. Men would eat first, followed by women, and then finally children. Also, the culture is full of sayings that reflect the degraded position of the women.[7]

Going out of the house was restricted for any woman. The father was the one who was responsible for shopping. However, during the pearling season, a woman had to go out, especially if she was

---

[5] Haya Al-Mughni, *Women in Kuwait The Politics of Gender*.(London: Saqi Books,2001) pp 67-94.

[6] Baqer Al-Najar, *AlMara' fe Alkhalej Alarabi wa Tahawelat Alhadatha Alaseera* (Women In the Arabian Peninsula). (Beirut: Al-Markaz Al-Thagafe Al-Arabi, 2000) pp 15-30.

[7] Ibid.

from low-class family who did not have maids to do their shopping for them.[8] A woman who went out a lot would be seen as wicked. Of course, no one would dare to go out unveiled. Small girls could play outside, but once they reached adolescence they could not leave the house until they were married.[9] Females got married at a very young age, sometimes even before reaching adolescence.[10] It was very common that a girl would never know that she was about to marry until a few hours before the wedding which took place that very same day.[11] Her opinion never mattered as long as her

---

[8] Al-Mughni, H. (2001) pp 44-5.

[9] There are two female sayings, which people at that time used in regards to women who went out of their house. The first 'A women should go out of her house only twice in her whole life; first when she goes to her husband house, and second when she goes to the grave. The other saying based on the fact that since women used to – and some still do– wear *Abaya* (The Abaya is a black overgarment worn by women in Muslim cultures, Wikipedia). Before a woman got married, her father would – sometimes – put a condition on the marriage saying "our daughter does not have an *Abaya*." Since a women – at that time – could not go out without it, it meant that the father did not want his daughter to go out of her husband's house at all.

[10] The Official Website of the State of Kuwait. *Al-Ta'leem fe Al-Kuwait Ghabl Ekteshaf Al-Naft (Education in Kuwait Before Oil Discovery)*. [online] [undated] Available from:
http://www.kuwait.kw/Diwan/main/Story_Of_Kuwait/Kuwait_before_Oil/Social_Life/education.html#WomanEdu11
[Accessed 5th Nov. 2004]

[11] Socio-economic cultural background of Kuwait.

father agreed;[12] many of girls got married to old men, to become widows while they were still in their early twenties.[13]

Some argue that economical factors helped to degrade women.[14] Since only males can work and earn money, they were the only ones who can take decisions in favour of their families. However, in some families women had to work as a seamstress, laundress or a housemaid, but this did not give much financial support since these were low income jobs.[15]

When oil was discovered, it affected the lifestyle of society deeply. After the discovery of oil, the principles of society, especially towards women, changed.[16] The Kuwaitis became more materialistic and society became modernized along the lines of Western societies. During the sixties, a new trend was established: for the first time some families started to send their daughters abroad to study.

---

[12]   In some cases the opinion of the groom too does not matter.
      The Official Website of the State of Kuwait. *Al-Ta'leem fe Al-Kuwait Ghabl Ekteshaf Al-Naft (Education in Kuwait Before Oil Discovery)*. [online] [undated] Available from:
      http://www.kuwait.kw/Diwan/main/Story Of Kuwait/Kuwait before Oil/ Social Life/education.html#WomanEdu11
      [Accessed 5th Nov. 2004]

[13]   In those days, if someone asked to marry a woman, it would be considered a disgrace to refuse his request – as long as he is known to have good-manners – regardless of his age or financial status for example.
      Socio-economic cultural background of Kuwait.

[14]   Al-Najar, B. (2000) pp 19

[15]   Ibid.

[16]   Oil was discovered in 1938, but the production of it did not start until 1950.

However, they were from very wealthy families who could afford such education and, at the same time, were open-minded families who had had the chance to socialise with people across cultures. Since the society was divided into different classes according to their financial status, women from the merchant class families did not socialise with the others.[17]

The women's movement in Kuwait did not start until the early sixties when two women's organizations were officially formed. However, Sabeeka Al-Najar argues that the women's movement started in the late forties when the women's education started to expand. Also in 1953, a group of women organised a seminar called '*Al-Hejab*' which demanded an end of the al-hejab era for all Kuwaiti women. Regardless of the fact that the news of this seminar was widely spread and created many different reactions, it did not have any effect in changing the social situation due to the extreme conservativeness of society at that time.[18]

The two organizations, which were formed in the sixties, represented two different points of views. The first organization was established in 1963 by a famous Kuwaiti activist called Nouria Al-Sadani who came from a middle-class family and did not have the chance to get her bachelor degree from abroad, unlike the members of the other

---

[17]   Al-Mughni, H. (2001) pp 67-94.

[18]   Sabeeka M. Al-Najar. Al-Haraka Al-Nesae'ya fe Al-Khaleej (Women's Movemen in the Gulf) In: Violet Dagher. *Al-Mara' wa Al-Osra fe Al-Mojtama't Al-Khaleejeya (Women and Family in the Gulf Societies).* (France: Editions Eurabe, 2004) pp 6-14.

organization. In the second organization, all the women were from the elite of the society and were highly educated from universities abroad. They refused to cooperate with Al-Sadani in establishing her organization. This was very disappointing to her because she was extremely optimistic that these women were in the minority; that very few such women had the chance to study abroad and gain an open-minded mentality.[19] As a result, Al-Sadani managed to find members for her organization who came from middle-class families just like herself.[20] This organization was called the Arab Women's Development Society (AWDS). The main objective of this society is to work to modernise women in different ways, but mainly by education. It was responsible for informing women – especially the Bedouins - how education is important for their lives.[21] The members of the organization believed that illiteracy is the main reason for women's subordination. They worked on the idea of 'modernizing' women from day one. They held different conferences with the purpose of enlightening women regarding the gender discrimination that all women are suffering from. The Society did some studies about social problems that effect women

---

[19] It might worth mentioning that when interviewing Nouria Al-Sadani and asked about this particular incident she did not want to comment on it, saying only that: Kuwaiti women have to focus more on their political rights (it was not given at that time). She added that if there was more co-operation such rights would have been passed in the seventies.

[20] Margret Badran. Kuwaiti Women in the Batlle: Before and After the Iraqi Occupation. In: *Islam, Gender and Social Changes*. (Amman: Al-Ahleyia, 2003) pp 364, 365.

[21] Sa'ad A. Al-Haji. *Al-Jame'yat Al-Nesae'ya Al-Ejtemae'ya* (Women's Cultural Societies).(1983) pp 798- 801.

such as divorce and polygamy it was one of the first studies in Kuwait. Such studies were represented at the Family Conference which was held in Kuwait in the early sixties.[22]

In 1971 the AWDS held a conference about the struggle of Kuwaiti women it was the first conference organised and directed for women. 100 Kuwaiti women participated in this conference which ended with a petition being handed to the President of the National Assembly. This petition strongly demanded both political and social rights for women. In 1973 the National Assembly discussed the demands of the petition for the first time since being founded in 1963.[23] The Islamists vehemently objected to the petition and expressed their opinions aggressively towards the leaders of the women's organizations. Their point of view was simply that the petition was against Islam. Although the Islamists failed to prove their point from the Quran or Hadith, they succeeded in preventing the demands of the petition from being carried out.[24]

The AWDS spent the '60s convincing women of the importance of education as an end for their struggle. Also, it tried to encourage women to participate in the public sphere which was dominated by

[22]   Al-Haji, S. (1983) pp 798- 801.

[23]   Dewan Al-Arab. *Nouria Al-Sadani.* [online] [29th July 2006] Available from: http://www.diwanalarab.com/spip.php?article5356&vo=56 [Accessed 1st May.2009]

[24]   Nouria Al-Sadani, *Almasera Altarekheya Lelheghogh Alseyaseya Lelmara' Alkwaytia* (History of Kuwaiti Women Suffrage Rights Movement). (Kuwait: Dar Al-Syasa, 1983) pp 54-59.

men. It organised some lectures and seminars about how important it was for the Kuwaiti women to participate in building up the country – especially since oil had just been discovered - and how it would benefit the country if it replaced the foreign workers with Kuwaiti women. In order to try to help the working mother, the AWDS opened the first nursery in Kuwait in 1967. It also honoured the very first women who participated in the public sphere in different activities with a generous celebration in order to set an example for the other women.[25]

As the AWDS worked on modernising and educating women and encouraging them to participate in public life, the objectives were shifted in the 70s. A major turning point occurred when Al-Sadani, the AWDS's leader was elected head of the Arab Family committee in 1971. This committee was part of the Arab Feminist Union lead by Huda Al-Sha'rawi, the famous Egyptian feminist. The new position gave support and was an endorsement of the Kuwaiti organization.[26]

When the petition was handed in 1973, although the Nationalists could not let the petition pass, they adopted women's political

---

[25]   Al-Mughni, H. (2001) pp 67-94.

[26]   Mentioned on the occasion of honouring Nouria Al-Sadani in the annual Kuwaiti cultural festival held by The National Council for Culture, Arts and Literature. The festival was called Qurain Cultural Festival and she was honoured in the eleventh year in Dec.2004.
Mahrajan Al-Qurain Al-Thaghafi (the Eleventh) Al-Quarain Cultural Festival. [online] [Dec.2004] Available from:
http://www.kuwaitculture.org/alqurain2004/taghderia.htm#book3-1
[Accessed 4th April. 2009]

rights as a part of their campaign for the next election. During this time, while a group of women activists held a campaign about 'equal rights', another group of women held an opposite campaign disagreeing with the enfranchisement of women.[27]

In 1974, the AWDS held another conference in favour of working women which came up with a list of recommendations for the betterment of the status of middle-class working women who did not have the chance to be university degree holders. In the same year, when the National Assembly was about to legislate the Family Law, the AWDS held seminars over one week and invited law specialists from across the Middle East in order to amend some of the articles that might affect some of the women's rights, for example the legal age of marriage. Another conference was held a year after in 1975 (the same year of the new election of the NA), focusing mainly on enfranchisement rights for women.[28]

The second women's organization was formed later on in 1963; this was the Women's Cultural and Social Society (WCSS). The organization was formed by a group of women who came from

---

[27]   Al-Mughni, H. (2001) pp 67-94. Also
      Al-Talea. *Annervarsy of the Human Rights Scociety.* [online] [29th June. 2005]
      Available from:
      http://www.taleea.com/newsdetails.php?id=4854&ISSUENO=1684
      [Accessed 4th Nov. 2006]

[28]   Al-Mughni, H. (2001) pp 67-94.

well known and upper-class families.[29] They represent a specific class of the society that are fortunate to have the chance to have a degree from universities abroad.[30] The idea behind establishing this society was to have an organization that can take care of women from poorer classes and housewives who did not have the chance to receive any education. Also, it was a good chance for its members to do some useful charitable work in their spare time. It might be worth mentioning that when that group of women presented their application to the Minister of Social Affairs and Labour, he rejected their application refusing the name of their society since they had put 'The Kuwaiti Women Club.' Describing the group as a 'club' did not fit the society, but he agreed after a month when they changed to the name to 'society'.[31]

The WCSS's membership was exclusive only to those who had a degree when most of women at that time were illiterate. Also, the activities provided by the society were exclusive to its members, so that the non-members cannot participate in those activities. As a result, only very few of selected women can enjoy both

---

[29] Mohammad Mansour. *Ba'd Najaheha Fe Ghadeyat Al-Mara' Al-Kuwaitia* (After The Success of Passing the Women's Suffrage Rights). [online] [2006] Available from:
http://www.ahl-alquran.com/arabic/show_article.php?main_id=373
[Accessed 4th Nov. 2008]

[30] Al-Mughni, H. (2001) pp 67-94.

[31] The Minister said that the description 'club' would create problems in the society especially since each member of those women – at that time – were studying abroad, Egypt, Lebanon and Scotland, so they might be accused of 'alienating the society'.
Al-Haji, S. (1983) pp 782.

membership and activities and who also came from the same merchant-class families (some of them were relatives). Although the WCSS participated in some charitable activities inside and outside Kuwait - most of the charities were for orphans -it did not make an effort to participate in problems that women suffered from during that period, such as violence against them.[32]

The WCSS held a conference in the Gulf region in 1975 as a response to the UN's declaration of the ' decade for women' from 1976 to 1985. All of the papers were presented by men, but they came with very important recommendations for equal opportunities and suffrage rights for women among their main demands.[33]

Women's political rights were in a truce between 1976 and 1982 when the Amir of Kuwait Sabah Salem Al-Sabah announced that the NA was dissolved. However, another conference was arranged in 1977 to discuss the status of the working women.

When the AWDS held the women's rights campaign, many of the merchant-class and members of the WCSS were against it. It was not because they were against the idea of enfranchising women, but because the AWDS was the one that was holding it. The WCSS did not like the attention that was paid to the

---

[32]   Al-Mughni, H. (2001) pp 67-94.

[33]   Nouria Al-Sadani. *Alharakat Alnesae'ya fe Algharn Aleshreen 1917-1981* (The Arabic Women's Movement in the 20th Century).(Kuwait, 1982) pp 37.

AWDS.[34] At that time another women's society was established called the Girl's Club, which as Mohammad Monsour argues was supported by Nouria Al-Sadani. The new society worked together with the AWDS to push the women's suffrage rights. The campaign gained greater importance when the two organizations worked together.[35]

In 1980 the Ministry of Social Affairs and Works dissolved the AWDS due to a violation of the condition of the number of board members.[36] Margret Badran argued that there are several reasons for closing this Society down. First, is the strong competion among the members that led to tension. Second, the connection between the Society and the nationalist activists in Egypt. Finally, the insistant demad for suffrage rights for women.[37]

There are some Islamic societies for women; in particular two were established in the early 1980s. However, their main activities were about giving Islamic teaching for the younger generations, and were not involved in politics.[38]Yet, the women's Islamic groups who represented the Shia approach had supported the women's suffrage rights. Khadeja Al-Mahmeed is one of the main activists

---

[34] Al-Mughni, H. (2001) pp 67-94.

[35] Mansour, M. (2006)

[36] Al-Sadani. *Alharakat Alnesae'ya fe Algharn Aleshreen 1917-1981.*(Kuwait, 1982) pp 37.

[37] Badran, M. (2003) pp 366.

[38] Al-Sadani, N. (1982) pp 39, 40.

who supported the women's rights issue and worked together with the WCSS in their campaign during the 1990s, unlike the women who represented the Sunni Islamic approach who tried to harm the suffragists' reputation.[39]

In 1982 a bill was presented by the MP Ahamad Al-Tukhaim to reform the Election Act to include women, but the bill was not passed. Although many of the MPs were in favour of the reform, they failed to vote. The WCSS and the Girls Club[40] handed a complaint to the National Assembly to reject the bill. The Girls Club established the Organizing Committee for the Political Rights for Kuwaiti Women. The Committee carried out some activities like fundraising, giving seminars, and writing articles regarding the issue. This was right before the 1985 election, though the next elected National Assembly was suspended a year after in 1986. Kuwait remained without any elected parliament until 1992 after the liberation from Iraq.[41]

On 1990 Kuwait was invaded by Iraqi troops. The occupation lasted for seven months. As it was dangerous for men to go out because of the possibility of getting arrested for no reason, it was left to the women to transfer money, obtain medicine, documents, and food. They also volunteered to undertake different jobs.

---

[39] Al-Mughni, H. (2001) pp 172-183. Also Mansour, M. (2006)

[40] A women's organization established in 1975. Health and sports for women were its main objectives.

[41] Al-Mughni, H. (2001) pp 143-145.

Although women had to fight the Iraqi occupation in armed resistance just like men, they protested in an all-female demonstration against the occupation, and were imprisoned and killed, still they were denied suffrage rights after Kuwait was liberated. As the women issue in Kuwait was an important one to the Western countries after Kuwait was liberated,[42] the Amir issued a decree giving women suffrage rights just like men; yet the decree was rejected by an all-male National Assembly.[43] The rejection was due to the fact that the Islamist movement made an alliance with the conservatives in order to defeat any initiation about women's rights.[44]

Regardless of the fact that there does not exist any text that forbad women from enfranchisement, Islamists were strict about it and insisted on rejecting it again in 2000 when it was presented by five liberals MPs by a 32-30 vote.[45] Some, such as Al-Mughni, argue that the bill did not pass because of shifting positions from some

[42] Ferry Biedermann. *The Struggle for Women's Rights in Kuwait.* [online] [26th April 2001] Available from:
http://www.rnw.nl/hotpots/html/kuwait01426.html.
[Accessed 2nd April.2009]

[43] 41:21 voted against it.
The New York Times. *Kuwait Rejects Political Rights for Women.* [online] [24th Nov.1999]Available from: http://chora.virtualave.net/kuwaitrejectswomen.htm
[Accessed 2nd March.2009]

[44] Al-Mughni, H. (2001) pp 155-6.

[45] CNN. *Kuwaiti liberals propose women's rights bill, again.* [online] [29th July 2000] Available from:
http://archives.cnn.com/2000/WORLD/meast/07/29/kuwait.women.rights.ap/index.html
[Accessed 2nd May.2009]

of the Liberals MPs who feared that women – if they were given the franchise rights – would vote for the Islamists representatives, though the bill was supported mainly by the liberals, Shia's, and the government members[46].Women tried to bring a case in the Constitutional Court several times in 2000 and 2001,[47] but all of them failed regarding a procedural cause.

In an interview, Nouria Al-sadani[48] stated that if Kuwaiti women had been united and more faithful to their main right, the enfranchisement right, they would have gained it a long time ago in the seventies.

In summary, the general examination here of the women's movement in Kuwait concludes that since its foundation it was not well organised and was unfocused in its main demands. Moreover, some of the women's organisations used it more as a position of prestige which led to a negative influence on the women's rights in general. As a result of both its attitude since it was founded and being representative of a specific class of society, the women's rights campaign led by the WCSS has only managed to annoy the majority of women. Seham Al-Fraih[49] concluded that there

---

[46] Al-Mughni, H. (2001) pp 175.

[47] Feminist Majority Foundation. *Kuwait*. [online] [undated] Available from: http://www.feminist.org/news/newsbyte/news_results.asp?us=1&glo. [Accessed 7th Feb.2009]

[48] Interview On Sunday 02-01-05.

[49] Arabic Language Professor in Kuwait University and Vice President of the Arab Organization for Human Rights.

is no women's movement in Kuwait; instead, there are a number of women who worked for the women's right sincerely. She also explained that the problem is that inside the women's groups there is tension which did not help in serving the women's cause in general– and suffrage rights specifically.[50]

Al-Sadani refers to nine reasons why the women's societies failed to serve the suffrage rights for women:

1. Lack of coordination between women's associations.
2. Fragmentation and disintegration of the women's movement in Kuwait.
3. Absence of the AWDS, one of the pillars of the family claim the rights of women.
4. Inexperience of the newly founded association such as the Girls Club.
5. The absence of proper planning programs for the women's societies to form lobby.
6. Failure to adopt a certain strategy for women's activities.
7. Absence of women from the sessions when the NA were discussing the suffrage rights.
8. Frustration that dominated the Arab nation during the 1970s and the 1980s.
9. The control that the religious trends had among people

---

[50]   Muddafar Abdulla. *Interview with Dr.Seham Al-Fraih.* [online] [3rd Aug.2005] Available from:
http://www.taleea.com/newsdetails.php?id=5214&ISSUENO=1689
[Accessed 8th Nov. 2006]

who opposed women's suffrage rights.[51]

Yet, as a result of the political upheaval that the whole region is going through, women were given the enfranchisement right in 2005 when the Election Act (35/1962) was amended to include women when it was exclusive to men. This is not as a result of the women's movement but the result of necessary political changes. Women practiced their full political rights as a candidate and as voters in 2006 for the first time. The ordinary parliament period in Kuwait is 4 years, but due to the repeated dissolve of the Parliament, women experienced their political rights three times from 2006 to 2009.

---

[51] Al-Najar, S. (2004).

3. THE WOMEN'S MOVEMENT IN EGYPT

Women in Egypt have a unique history regarding the Pharaohs period. During that time women became queens like Cleopatra and Hatshepsut, ruling as wisely and fairly as any male king. However, as time passed, different factors changed the position of women.[52]

---

[52]   Aida Beshara. *The Role of Women in Integrated Development in Egypt.*(London: State University of New York Press, 1987) pp 337-343.

Egypt was one of the first countries in the Middle East to open schools for girls when Mohammad Ali Pasha was the Ruler: education and modernization was one of his main concerns.[53] Also, many of the important thinkers who demanded women's liberation were Egyptians, like Muhammad Abdu, Qasem Amin, and Jamal-Aldain Al-Afgani. The main demands were for education and the right to have a job for women. Those researchers' thoughts were direct motivation for the women's movement later on.[54] Furthermore, the early move in allowing students to study abroad helped to gain more liberal attitudes towards women.[55]

During the mid-nineteenth century, Mohamed Ali Pasha was the ruler of Egypt. He was known as an open-minded person and liked to westernise the country. He asked for a French doctor named Dr. Antonio-Barthelemy Clot to establish a new medical system in the country. One of the schools the French doctor had established was the 'School of Midwives' in 1832. This was the first school of its kind to teach girls all about obstetrics skills. To graduate it took a full six years of study, and the graduates were referred to not only as midwives but as doctors. This move enabled

---

[53] Ayad Al-Qazzat. *Education of Women in the Arab World.* [online] [undated] Available from:
http://www.library.cornell.edu/colldev/mideast/awomeduc.htm
[Accessed 14th June. 2009]

[54] Nadje Al-Ali. *Secularism, Gender and the State in the Middle East.* (Cambridge: University Press, 2000) pp 56-60.

[55] Dr.Latefa Salem. *Al-Mara' Al-Masreya wa Al-Tagyer Al-Ejtemae' 1919-1945* Egyptian Women and Social Changes 1919-1945). (Cairo: Al-Haya' Al-Masreya Al-Amma lelketab, 1984) pp 14-21.

the Egyptian women to demand their rights and liberties before any other women in the Middle East.[56] The main problem that the founders faced was to find students. At that time it was not proper for girls to go to schools, especially a professional school. The problem was solved by bringing females from the slave market, or orphans.[57]

The women's movement in Egypt started by the end of the nineteenth century[58] when different voluntary women's organizations were established. Egypt was under the Ottoman Empire at that time. Egypt joined the Empire in 1517. As the Ottoman rule in Egypt lasted for many centuries it has affected the Egyptians in general and women in specific. The term *harem* appeared during that period. The term refers to upper-class women and means the seclusion of women.[59] The Turks exhibited cruel and tyrannical behaviour towards women, not only to the Turkish women living in Egypt but to all Egyptian women, to the extent that it became part of their own customs and their way of living. However, things started to change when Great Britain occupied Egypt.[60]

---

[56]   Laila Abu-Lughod. *Remaking Women*. (Princeton, N.J.: Princeton University Press, 1998) pp 35-63.

[57]   Ibid.

[58]   Beth Baron. *The Women's Awakening in Egypt*. (London: Yale University Press, 1994) pp 168-175.

[59]   Majda S. Makhlouf. *Al-Harem fe Al-Ghasr Al-Othmani* (The Harem in the Othman Palace). (Cairo: Dar Al-Afagh Al-Arabeyia, 1998) pp 10-18.

[60]   Soha Abdel-Kader. *Egyptian Women in Changing Society, 1899-1987.* (Colorado: Lynne Rienner Publishers,Inc,1987) pp 1-23.

Women played a major role in the 1919 revolution; they succeeded in showing the nation in general that they can change and affect the destination of their country. They protested, went on strike, and boycotted English products in order to support the independency of Egypt. A few ladies' names appeared, but one of the most important was Huda Sha'rawi who was the first to organise a protest that included more than 500 ladies. Sha'rawi had formed more than one women's society which was involved in politics and mainly in supporting the struggle against the British occupation. Also, Safeya Zaglol, Sa'ad Zaglol's wife (the leader of Al-Wafd Party which led the major struggle for independency at that time) had such an effect on much of Egyptian life by standing sincerely beside her husband that they called her 'mother of the Egyptians'. Moreover, the Wafd members continued to ask Safeya for her opinion in the party's matters even after her husband's death. Although there were many women who had the courage to stand up for their beliefs against the imperialists and their supporters, the motion for women's political rights failed in 1944, just like the motion of the right for women to be members in the senate had failed in 1938 after the strong participation for women against the 1936 treaty.[61] Women did not achieve political rights until 1956.[62] It is worth mentioning that Sha'rawi did not became famous from

---

[61] The Treaty agreed to end the British military occupation, yet to keep the British army in some designated areas.

[62] Ahmad Taha. *Almara' Kefahoha wa Amaloha* (Woman: their Strugele and Hope). (Cairo: Dar Al-Jmaheer, 1964) pp 71-73.
Amal Al-Sabki. *Alharaka Alnesae'ya fe Maser* (Women's Movement in Egypt). (Eygpt: Al-Haya' Al-Mesreya Al-Amman Lel-Ketab, 1986) pp 106.

only participating in the revolution, but also due to the fact that she was the first one to go unveiled in public right after she came from a conference in Rome in 1923. When the ship arrived in dock, everybody was shocked that there was a lady who was not wearing anything to cover her face. Zaglol congratulated her, and ask his wife to do the same, but she preferred not to. After this, many women followed Sha'rawi and went unveiled in public.[63]

Women's societies started after WW1. Most of them worked on social and political aspects since Egypt – at that time – was full of major political change. From the very early 1920s women demanded to be equal with men, and to be liberated when Huda Sha'rawi was the leader of the Al-Wafd party (the women's subdivision), and then when she formed the leader of the Egyptian Feminist Union (EFU) – after quitting from Al-Wafd.[64]

The EFU had certain demands which were written in its constitution. The major demands were:

1. Equal educational opportunity for women.
2. Raising the age for marriage.
3. Reform of the marriage procedures (many females were forced to get married).
4. The government should pay more attention to the public health and to children (the infant death rates were very

---

[63]   Al-Sabki, A. (1986) pp 26-45.

[64]   Al-Sabki, A. (1986) pp 26-45.

high at that time).[65]

Also, another demand for the Union that Sha'rawi worked on is the reform of the Family Law that Egypt had in that period of time. In 1935, she gave a lecture on polygamy. Her main demand was for the government to ban it.[66]

In 1923 the Union worked with the women's branch of the Wafd Party, and came up with a declaration with all of these demands addressed to all international and national organizations. Moreover, they organized a protest and raised banners with their demands and marched to the Parliament.[67]

Following this, there were different women's organizations all over Egypt. A distinguished union established right before the end of WW2 was called the National Women Party. This was formed by Fatima Ne'mat and all the members were lawyers. They demanded that women should be equal with men by accepting females in every university department and in every job position (there were many jobs that were forbidden to women); allowing them to be members in all of the unions; banning polygamy; restricting men the freedom to divorce; increasing the divorce allowance; and

---

[65]   Huda Sha'rawi. *Auto-biography of Huda Sha'rawi.* (Syria: Al-Mada House, 2003) pp 217. Also Jouslin H. Al-Debs. *Huda Sha'rawi.* [online] [6th Mar.2004] Available from: http://www.daralhayat.com/society/03-2004/20040305-06p18-01.txt/story.html [Accessed 8th Nov. 2004]

[66]   Leila Ahmad. Early Feminism Movements in The ME. In: *Muslim Women.* (Australia: Croom Helm Australia Pty Ltd., 1984) pp 119.

[67]   Taha,A. (1964) pp 71-73.

the raising of the custody age of children in order to stay longer with their mothers before transferring the custody right to the father.[68]

Before 1921, education for girls used to be provided by the colonials only, and for a certain class of people. Those in the upper-class believed in the importance of education for girls, but they would rather have tutors at home. On the other hand, the middle-class people did not mind their daughters going to schools paying for tuition so that their daughters would not socialise with lower-class girls.[69]

Nabaweya Mosa established a school for girls: the 'Developing Egyptian Girls Society' which was the first Arabic school for girls in early 1921. In 1923 a group of members on the Egyptian Feminist Union went to the Prime Minister at that time asking for elementary and high schools for girls. Their demand was welcomed and provided. In the early 1930s, education became compulsory for girls.[70]

Higher education did not start until later when Ahmad Lotfi AlSayed the Head of the Fuad's University, believed that women have an equal right to get a higher education just like men. He worked on it secretly with the Deans of the Literature and the

---

[68]   Dr. Salem, L. (1984) pp 52-65.

[69]   Baron,B. (1994) pp 122-126.

[70]   Ruth F. Woodsmall. *Moslem Women Enter A New World.* (NY: AMS Press, 1975) pp 184. Also Dr.Salem, L. (1984) pp 52-65.

Medical Schools. Without informing the media or the ministry, 17 girls were admitted in four schools in 1929. That incident raised a major argument because admitting girls to the university means girls socialising with boys, bringing the possibility of depravity. The argument did not stand for a long. On the contrary, the number of girls attending the university greatly increased year after year. In 1937, there was a strong movement towards banning co-education in the university, but that attitude could not stand when it was strongly resisted by the students and the liberalists. Instead, the uniform issue was presented, but again the college girls' student rejected the idea, and conservatives could not impose it.[71]

Although the 1919 revolution was known to be the main corner of women's movement in Egypt, some argue that the women's movement had started long before then, and women's participation in that revolution was not a sudden action for women. Women had supported Ahmad Orabi in his battle against the Turks (1875-1882[72]) and they had raised funds. Even the princes believed in Orabi, although he was fighting against King Khedewi Tawfeegh.

---

[71]   Dr.Salem, L. (1984) pp 72-97.

[72]   Arab News. *Birth of Ahmad Orabi (A Revolutionary Leader)*.[online] [31st Mar.2001] Available from:
        http://www.arabicnews.com/ansub/Daily/Day/010331/2001033136.html
        [Accessed 28th May.2009]

At that time many important thinkers who believed in women's liberation as a way for any nation to be developed appeared. Also, it was the time of the famous female poet, Aisha Taimour, who had first appeared in 1869.[73] After that, the female press started to develop. By 1913 there were more than nine magazines edited by women and addressed to women.[74] One of the most important thinkers who daringly issued a book called the *Liberation of Women* was Qasim Amin. What helped Amin to have a liberated view about women and to have the guts to issue these views in a book was his education in France. Amin was specific in his demands towards women:

1. Get rid of the veil.
2. Education for women.
3. Men have the right to divorce – according to Sharia- but it has to be conditioned.
4. Polygamy should be banned unless there was an extreme need for that.

---

[73] Al-Sabki, A. (1986) pp 13-16. Also Nabeela Hashim. *Aisha Al-Taimouriya*. [online] [undated] Available from:
http://cmadp.com/taymur.htm
[Accessed 8th Nov.2004]

[74] Kareema Hasan. *Rae'dat Sahafeyat mn Zamin Fat* (Journalists Women in the Passed Decades). [online] [14th April.2006] Available from:
http://harakamasria.org/node/5719
[Accessed 8th March.2009]. Also for more details on women's press in Egypt: Beth Baron. *The Women's Awakening in Egypt*.(New York: Yale University, 1994) pp 13- 37.

5. Women should have the right to have a job.[75]

It was not easy for the society to even listen to such demands. As a result, Amin was accused of many things, including the accusation that he was an atheist.[76] In spite of the strong objection against Amin, he continued to spread his thoughts about women and tried to make society acknowledge the importance of liberating women. Lots of men felt threatened by these thoughts because they were aware of how they might lose control over women if such thoughts were publicized.

Amin was strongly against polygamy, and tried to prove that it is against human nature and that it can only result in hatred within the family and brothers from different mothers despite the financial issue.[77] Furthermore, Amin related the backwardness of the ME then compared to the rest of the world – especially the West – who were progressing, the status of women. He concluded that a nation would be measured from the way they treat women;

---

[75] Mohammad Emara (Islam online website). *Qasim Amin*. [online] [undated] Available from:
http://www.islamonline.net/Arabic/history/1422/06/article19a.shtml
[Accessed 7th Feb.2009]. Also Fat'hi Aamer. *Qasim Amin fe Mahakim Al-taftesh* (Qasim Amin in Inquisitions).[online] [19th Dec.2004] Available from:
http://www.al-araby.com/articles/939/041219-939-pnp01.htm
[Accessed 7th Feb.2006]

[76] Al-Sabki, A. (1986) pp 13-16.

[77] Emara, M.

a measure of whether it is civilized nation or not.[78] Sa'ad Zaglol gave support to Amin, though this meant that he was risking his leadership. As already mentioned, Zaglol encouraged his wife to go in public unveiled in order to set an example for all Egyptian ladies.[79] Also, through its leader, Sha'rawi, the EFU founder, supported the same ideas that Amin demanded for women.[80] Also, it demanded a family law – when there was not any – to protect the status of women in different cases especially in divorce. They sought for women to have the right to divorce her husband just as men can. The Union demanded that the average age for marriage should be raised, 16 for girls and 18 for boys.[81] The Union raised this demand in June 1923 to the Prime Minister. Later on in the same year, the King issued a decree limiting the marriage age as the Union demanded. However, that decree has produced different problems of how people abused the law especially in the countryside. Although there were a lot of loopholes in the law, it achieved a little of its purpose, and this was important for the women's movement.[82]

---

[78] Ulil Abdulla. *Islam, Women, and Heresy.* [online] [24th Oct.2003] Available from:
      http://www.umich-cseas.org/eventsandnews/abstracts/ULIL/Third%20talk.htm
      [Accessed 8th June.2009]

[79] Mamdoh Esmae'l. *Al-Hejab wa Ma'rakat Al-Tagreeb* (The Veil and the Battle of
      Westernization). [online] [16th Jan.2004] Available from:
      http://al-shaab.org/GIF/16-01-2004/c1.htm
      [Accessed 8th June.2009]

[80] Sha'rawi,H. pp 243,244, 329- 334. Also, Al-Sabki, A. pp 13-16.

[81] Al-Sabki, A. (1986) pp 13-16.

[82] Dr. Salem, L. (1984) pp 14-21.

What helped Sha'rawi in her quest is that she came from a wealthy family, so she was not in need of any financial support. When she first travelled to the West, she noticed that they had a stereotyped idea about how backward women were in the Middle East in general. As a result, she decided to publish a journal in French –a language she was fluent in - in order to correct this idea. The journal started in 1925 and only stopped in 1940 due to WW2. Sha'rawi made efforts to send the paper free of charge to all foreign organizations in Egypt.[83]

By the time of the death of Sha'rawi in 1947, the EFU had turned its attention to become once more a social and charity institution rather than a political organisation.[84]

By the end of WW2, things had changed. The number of working women in both industry and business sectors had increased. Socialism had started to find its way in the country. As it was the time when citizens were fighting strongly for independency, women participated in a great deal just like men. Two women's societies were established during that time: the Women's Party leaded by Fatima Rashid in 1942 and the Daughter of the Nile

---

[83]   Taha,A. (1964) pp 65-66.

[84]   Abdel-Kader, S. (1987) pp 108.

organization was established in 1949 by Dr. Dureya Shafeq.[85] One of the main aims for both societies was the demand for equal rights for women. Women were very active by this stage. They participated in every strike against imperialism. Moreover, they participated in carrying weapons. A woman was liable to be killed and poisoned by the colonists just like a man.[86] Women succeeded in becoming members in some of the labour unions.

The 1952 Revolution, led by Jamal Abdul-Naser, was important for women. Since the activists for revolution were inspired by communism, they believed in equal rights among citizens - men *and* women. It was because of this revolution that women got political rights in the 1956 constitution. In the 1957 election, two women were elected and one appointed as a minister for the Social and Work Affairs Ministry. Women earned more rights as a worker afterwards.[87]

---

[85] Dureya Shafeq was one of the most famous women's activists at that time. She believed in the women's cause from different aspects: Socially (when she worked to change the Family Law to provide more protection for women especially in regards to divorce); politically (She turned her society into a political party after the revolution, to be the first political party established by a woman); and economically (when she organised a huge demonstration with 1500 people to storm the Parliament forcing them to discuss the women's demands especially the issue of equal payment between men and women).
Women Literature Assosation of UAE. *Dureya Shafeq*.[online] [26th Oct.2004] Available from:
http://www.alrabetta.ae/content/view/854/89/
[Accessed 14th June.2009]

[86] Taha,A. (1964) pp 85-103.

[87] Majed Badran. *Ahwal Alnesa' fe Masr* (Women's Conditions in Egypt). (Cairo: Dar Aldewan,1996) pp 44-50.

The Revolution believed in the ability of women as powerful workers. Different laws were set in place to insure women in the workplace. This succeeded in raising their numbers in the industrial sector: from 3.3% in 1961 to 13% in 1976. The Charter of 1961 announced that: 'women have to be equal to men, she has to be free from all of the obstacles in order to take her place in the society.' Women participated in a very large numbers in industry sector to the extent that there were 200 000 women unionists out of 100 000 0000 members in 1970s. Although it was decided to dismiss all the parties in the country in 1953 and only keep the Socialism Arab Union - the ruling party - women succeeded in becoming members: there were seven members of parliament in 1971.[88]

When the government dissolved all the political parties in order to follow the one party system, it affected the rights of women. It is noteworthy that Shafeq, the founder of 'Daughter of the Nile', tried to fight that decision for the sake of democracy and the rights of women, but this was ended when she became a prisoner in her own house and when all the publishing media she owned were closed.[89]

Although the 1952 Revolution gave women lots of rights, like education, work, and equality treatment, it failed to give women

---

[88]   Abdel Kader, S. (1987) pp 112-115.

[89]   Amani Saleh. *Women in Modern Culture and Society: A Century of Arabic Discourse.* (Demascus: Dar Al-Fik, 2002) pp 88-92.

the right of free speech and banned her from expressing herself and the demands for rights.[90]

The country had started a new strategy by the 70s. It accepted the idea of multiparty, so it allowed the establishment of parties other than the ruler party which used to be the only one in the country. By then women had gain lots of benefits as a result of what the 1952 Revolution gave her. The participation of women was very high in different jobs. [91] During that period, the fundamentalist Islamists appeared and made women their main bone of contention. They made several demands, but most importantly:

1. Women should return to her private sphere, only men can participate in the public sphere.
2. The interaction between the sexes is totally forbidden.
3. The husband has the right of the control over his family; the wife should only obey.
4. Only the husband has the right to take every single decision in the family matters including the absolute authority of divorce.
5. Women should not go out unveiled.[92]

---

[90]   Saleh. A. (2002) pp 8892.

[91]   Saleh. A. (2002) pp 88-92.

[92]   Abdul-Kareem Sulaiman. *Al-Islameyon wa Al-Mara'* (Woman and the Islamists). [online] [2nd July.2004] Available from:
http://www.rezgar.com/debat/show.art.asp?aid=20159
[Accessed 14th June.2009]

These demands would return women to a position that she was in before the 1919 Revolution when she fought a lot for her liberty from all of these restrictions. Another wave is the secularism movement which took a position against fundamentalism. A lot of women joined this movement as they were aware of the dangers of the fundamentalist ideas if they were to be applied. Some of the members of secularism accused religion to be the reason for women's backward position. Because those two movements were too extreme, a mid-way Islamic wave appeared in order to come up with moderate thoughts towards women.[93]

To conclude, liberation was the priority for the Egyptian woman. She fought against colonialism in every possible way. The women's organizations, although different in their main objectives, were more focused and clear in their approach. Despite the fact that there were many liberals who believed in women's rights since the nineteenth century and the long years of fighting, women did not gain their political right until the middle of the last century.

---

[93]   Saleh. A. (2002) pp 88-92.

4. The Women's Movement in Iran

The position of Iranian women was not very different from that of women in Egypt. The restrictions on women's freedom to go in public and the veiling issue were the same. Back in the late 18th and early 19th century, Literature and poetry were the only domains in which woman could express herself. Whereas village women enjoyed some freedoms, the urban women did not. Furthermore, it depended on the social class, so that the restrictions increased on women from upper-class families.[94] However, Haleh Esfandiari

---

[94]   Farah Azari. *Women of Iran*. (London: Ithaca Press London, 1983) pp 170-88.

argued that even though the women in the village were able to move more freely, they suffered not only from the hard labour, but also from a complete control of their lives by their husbands who were free to marry up to four wives and could have an unlimited number of 'temporary wives'.[95] Although education for girls was introduced very early in 1835 by the Americans, the main condition the government imposed is that it could not be applied to Muslim girls.[96]

However, forty years later, when the first school was opened, Muslim girls were allowed to go to school. Yet it remained the first and only school for girls until the beginning of the twentieth century when there were 50 schools in 1910 in Tehran.[97] Literacy for women used to be seen as a dangerous thing and against Islam. Some had believed the creation of a women's mind prevented her from accepting any knowledge[98]. Traditionalists and religious people tried to attack girls' schools in different ways. When Tuba Azmudeh established a school in 1907, the government declared it was not responsible for the safety of the girls. As they left school, they were harassed or called prostitutes. Some parents who believed

---

[95] The Shia Sect which make up the majority of the Iranian population, have what is called 'Mota'a' Marriage which is a temporary marriage. It will be discussed in greater detail in chapter five.

[96] Haleh Esfandiari. *Reconstructed Lives*. (Washington DC: The Woodrow Wilson Centre Press,1997) pp 20,21.

[97] Azari, A. (1983) pp 170-88.

[98] Eliz Sanasarian. *The Women's Rights Movement in Iran*. (New York: praege Publishers, 1982) pp 4-13.

in education for their daughters decided to hire home tutors in order to protect their children from being attacked.[99]

Looking at the modern history of Iran, there were four major ruling phases. First, there was the Qajars whose ruling period ended in the early years of the twentieth century. Second, the Constitutional Revolution took place at that time and supported some of women's rights. Then, the Pahlavi Revolution occurred in 1925; it was an important period for a woman since she gained a major degree of her freedom. The final stage was the Khomeini Revolution in 1979, which was about fundamentalism.[100]

During the Qajars period, women were isolated and prevented from going out alone. In both the private and public spheres there was segregation. Even on the pavements of the streets, there were designated pavements for men and others for women.[101]

The women's position in Iran during that period was not very different from that in any other ME country. In spite of that fact, there was some participation of women in politics and in social aspects of society. Tajol-Saltaneh was a writer and poet. Her education in Persian and French literature gave her the ability to

---

[99] Ibid, pp 39.

[100] Camron Amin. *The Making of the Modern Iranian Women.* (Florida: University Press of Florida, 2002) pp 1-12. Also
Nikki R. Keddie. *Women in Iran Since 1979.* [online] [2000] Available from: http://www.iranchamber.com/society/articles/women_iran_since_1979.php [Accessed 10th June. 2009]

[101] Sanasarian, E. (1982) pp 4-13.

explore other cultures and to compare them with her own. She criticized the position of Iranian women by explaining how veiling was a major obstacle to their freedom. Her view was that if Iranian women cannot be like European women, then at least she has to have the same rights as women who live in the villages. The urban women work freely in the fields without veiling.[102]

A major factor for Iranian women's movement was the Constitutional Revolution in which education for girls was one of its main results. This revolution took place in the early years of the twentieth century. Iranians protested against the dictatorship led by Qajars. Women played a major role in the protests: they helped to build up the National Bank of Iran by selling their jewellery, so that the government would not have to borrow money from any foreign countries. Also, they carried guns and fought in protection of the revolutionaries. Not only that, but they also showed a great courage fighting against the Russian-British agreement to divide Iran between them.[103]

Since this Revolution, women started to form organizations and publications for themselves. Unlike the men's, their social and political activities were separate. The main purpose for these kinds of activities was the position of women in Iran. Regardless of the fact that women had strongly participated in the Revolution to impose the constitution that included the embitterment situation

---

[102]   Azari, F. (1983) pp 170-188.

[103]   Azari, F. (1983) pp 170-188.

for women, it had very disappointing results for women. Since the Islamic influence was high at that period, it did not help a lot to change women's position. On the contrary, it was seen that women's participation was only exceptional and happened because of certain circumstances, and now she should go back to her own place: the home. Although women gained some rights after the Revolution, many other rights were denied. She was still evaluated as an object for sex and love only, and she would never be equal to men.[104] She struggled and fought in order to have a constitution to give Iranian democracy. This happened particularly when it was too dangerous for men to go outside, so women were the ones who transferred guns and news. However, she was paid back by the denial of her political rights in the first formed parliament after imposing the constitution.[105]

In 1925, Reza Shah took over; he wanted to modernise the country which had been affected by Attaturk in Turkey. Although the new government had closed all existing organizations including the women's, it believed in the importance of women in general. One of the most important laws that affected all of Iranian women was the 'Unveiling Law'. In 1936, the law was presented to prevent women from wearing a veil by force since it was symbolic of the

---

[104] Parvin Paidar. *Women and the political process in the twentieth-century Iran*. (New York: Cambridge University Press, 1995) pp 50-77. Also Azari, F. (1983) pp 170-188.

[105] Homa Hoodfar. *The Women's Movement in Iran*. [online] [1999] Available from: http://www.iranchamber.com/society/articles/women_secularization_ islamization1.php
[Accessed 3rd June. 2009]

traditionalism which was – according to the Shah's view - against modernisation and westernisation.[106]

During that period, one of the important organizations established in 1944 was 'Our Awaking'. It represented Communist thoughts. Beside, demanding equal and political rights for women, the main objectives for the organization was to improve working women's lives by demanding more rights for them. Although the organization represented Communism and was affected by the Russian Peace Movement, nationalising the south oil fields was its priority. It participated in many activities in order to support Mossadegh's move towards this purpose. During that period there were different organizations and societies for women. Ashraf, the Shah's twin sister, decided to unite all of the women's organizations into one called The High Council of Women. Each organization continued to do its activities, but under regime control.[107]

After the coup d'etat on Mossadegh, the period from 1953-1963 was not a good one for democracy since all political activity was abolished, and all of the organizations were closed down. During that time, the country had a lot of strikes and demonstrations against governmental procedures in banishing all of the political activities. Women, from different classes and careers, and even students, participated in the protest. Some of them were killed because of that; the famous poet Marzieh Oskoui was one of these.

---

[106] Asghar Fathi. *Women and the Family in Iran.* (Netherlands: E.J. Brill, 1985) pp 107-112.

[107] Amin, C. (2002) pp 189-201. Also, Azari, F. (1983) pp 170-188.

When Mohammad Reza Pahlavi arrived by a white revolution, it was an important period for women. The new Shah gave women the political rights that she had been struggling for and had demanded for years. Women then were able to vote and be members in the parliament just like men in 1962. The Shah assigned two women in the Senate and, most importantly, issued the Family Protection Law in 1967. Women during the regime of the new Shah were allowed to wear the veil.[108]

Later on, protests against the dictatorship of the Shah started to increase. Two main protest groups were formed undercover: the Mojahedeen and the Fedae'en. The first group formed in 1963 and has an Islamic approach. However, the other group, which was established when it made its first attack in 1970, represented Marxist thought.[109] Both groups believed in armed protest and, more importantly, both of them included women members. Women's participation within the two groups was magnificent. Many of them were arrested, imprisoned, and killed for their cause. Iranian people saw the Shah as an agent for imperialism;

---

[108]   Esfandiari, H. pp 19-28.

[109]   Dr. Zayar. *The Iranian Revolution- Past, Present and Future.* [online] [undated] Available from:
http://www.marxist.com/the-iranian-revolution-past-present-future.htm
[Accessed 12th June.2009]. Also, for more about the communism movement in Iran, see the interview with Ayman Bydar, jourmalist in The Anarki Comminist Magazine:
Mark, Arya and Robin. *Anarki in Iran.* [online] [19th Sep.2005] Available from:
http://www.kefaya.org/05znet/051005baymenbidar.htm
[Accessed 10th June.2009]

they fought against him in different ways, and women had a part in every kind of protest.[110]

When the 1979 Revolution took place, it brought about a totally different attitude towards women. As soon as the fundamentalists took over, different rumours started to spread all around the country. These were about women and women's rights. The new government saw that some of Shah's rules must be changed to suit Islam and its ethics. Some Islamists who took over the Ministry of Judgment started a campaign against appointing women as judges, and cancelled the training programme for female law graduates. Also, they intended to change the Family Protection Act. Furthermore, there was some reconsideration about the compulsory veiling.[111] Within less than a month the Revolutionists started to attack some of the women's rights leading to the formation of the Association of Women Lawyers to try to stop any procedures against women's rights. The Association organized a rally on 8 March, which happened to be International Women's Day. 15 000 women gathered to start marching on the streets; the number of protesters rose to reach to 30 000 women. Although the event succeeded in drawing the media's attention from around the world, Iranian media described these ladies with different, improper accusations. Out of anger, these women

---

[110]   Azari, F. (1983) pp 170-188.

[111]   Mehrangiz Kar. *The Legal Status of Iranian Women.*[online] [18th April 2000]
Available from:
http://www.iranian.com/Opinion/2000/April/Women/
[Accessed 17th June.2009]

decided to march again for three days, but were harassed in every possible way which prevented them from making the third day. The following day they were also attacked harshly by the media and described as 'Western dolls', traitors acting for the West, and other terrible descriptions.[112] As a response to the protest, the government promised to work on equal rights, and that there would be no intention of a compulsory veiling law. However, the day after, March 9th, the government called for segregations in all sports activities, which meant that women could no longer participate in any international sports activities. This resulted in another massive demonstration the day after, where women were beaten by armed fundamentalists.[113] Due to the fact that the regime was attacking every Western tradition, International Women's Day was seen as one of the most dangerous traditions that the republic should get rid of. As a result, it was announced that 7 May was the new Women's Day. This date was the birthday of Fatima, the daughter of the Prophet Muhammad, who the Shia Muslims view as having an extraordinary personality and should be the ideal for every Muslim woman.[114]

---

[112]   Esfandiari, H. (1997) pp 19-20.

[113]   Pedram Missaghi. *First protests against mandatory hijab.*[online] [7th March 2000] Available from:
http://www.iranian.com/History/2000/March/Women/index.html
[Accessed 17th June.2009]

[114]   The Institute for compilation and Publication of Imam Khomeini's Work. *The Position of Women From the Viewpoint of Imam Khomeini.*[online] [2001] Available from:
http://www.iranchamber.com/history/rkhomeini/books/women_position_khomeini.pdf
[Accessed 20th June.2009]. Also:Azari, F. (1983) pp 190-224.

As the Revolution adopted Islam ideology, it was increasingly difficult for representatives on the left to proceed with their activities.[115] At that time, there were different women's organizations which represented different political views. There were organizations which presented the left wing, as well as the right wing which was supported by the regime. There were two publications for women who supported Marxism: *Equality* and *Women in Struggle.* But these publications were forced to work undercover. There were many protests and demonstrations against censorship, imprisonment, and demands for the freedom of speech.[116]

On the other hand, Revolutionists had changed some laws that led to two of women's organizations, the National Union of Women and Women's Emancipation, to set up the Women's Solidarity Committee in order to find solutions to stop the violation of women's rights.[117] The new government had lowered the female

---

[115]   Other than joining the political organizations, many women joined the armed struggle against the government and also the 'underground political activity' - especially the groups who represent the leftist.
Hammed Shahidian. Women and Clandestine Politics in Iran, 1970-1985. *Feminist Studies.* 1997, 23 (1), pp 7-42.

[116]   Azari, F. (1983) pp 190-224. Also
Azar Tabari. The Women's Movement in Iran: A Hopeful Prognosis. *Feminist Studies.* 1986, 12 (2), pp 342-360.

[117]   Azari, F. (1983) pp 190-224. Hoodfar, H. (1999)

age for marriage from 18 to 13,[118] banned married girls from attending secondary schools, and limited the opportunities for jobs, education, and sports for females.[119] The Committee arranged a conference which succeeded in drawing the attention for women's struggle, especially with the new laws. After that, the Committee arranged another rally which also took place on 8 March 1980. It is noteworthy that both organizations represented the left wing, and were affected by the Fedayeen group which was dissolved in the early days of the revolution. In July 1980, a new law was published banning any female employee from attending work without the *hejab* (scarf). Feeling that their position was going backwards, there were spontaneous demonstrations the day after in front of the Prime Minister's office. Both NUW and WE leaders handed a resolution of three major demands:

---

[118] The changes to the Family Law were major since the previous Law – during the Pahlavi Era – it was more Westernized for instance the divorce grounds were the same for both men and women. Men cannot divorce their women as they wish – as in the Sharia Law states. Men also have to file a divorce suit just like women. The marriage age was 20 for men, and 18 for women. This used to be considered one of the highest ages in Family Law in the region. Finally, women have the right to seek custody of their children where it used to be guaranteed to the father. These were the major changes to the law, in addition there were also some other minor changes in regards to polygamy and temporary marriage for example.
Patricia J. Higgins. Women in the Islamic Republic of Iran. *Journal of Women in Culture and Society.* 1985, 10 (3), 477-494.

[119] In fact, these are just examples, the changes are longer list.
Mehrangiz Kar. *The Legal Status of Iranian Women.* [online] [2004] Available from: http://www.iranchamber.com/podium/society/041127_legal_status_iranian_women.php
[Accessed 17th June. 2009]
For more details about the changes:
Val Moghadam. Revolution, the State, Islam, and Women. *Social Text.* 1989, 22, pp 40-61.

1. Changing the marriage and divorce laws.
2. Equal opportunities with men in education and jobs.
3. The veil should remain optional.[120]

None of these demands were looked at; on the contrary, any women who went unveiled would be harassed and the assaulter would get away with it. Harassment would start from throwing stones to knife attacks. Also, many of women were fired from their jobs with different excuses. Some of the left wing parties that still retained their own publications and tried to support women and write about their harassment but it did not change the situation.[121]

Some of the Women's Organization sources formed an alliance called the Muslim Women's Movement (MWM). Its main object was to promote the revolution and its new regime. One of the active women was Azam Taleghani who also established the Society of Women for the Islamic Revolution after leaving the MWM. It was common to find a women organization in every profession which usually started with the word 'Muslim'.[122]

As women lost many of the rights that they had gained before many organizations, societies and publications were formed in

---

[120] Azari, F. (1983) pp 190-224.

[121] Paidar, P. (1995) 234-236.

[122] Ali A. Mahdi. The Iranian Women's Movement: A Century Long Struggle. *The Muslim World*. Oct. 2004, 94 (4), pp 427-448. Also
Azari, F. (1983) pp 190-224. Also, Paidar, P. (1995) pp 237-242.

order to speak on women's behalf. However, the Association of Women Lawyers was the most active and it is the only one that still exists. In 1980, all political parties were banned, which meant that there were a lot of arrests and executions. This led to some organizations being formed outside Iran like the National Union of Women and National Council of Resistance.[123]

On the other hand, accompanying the Revolution, the Islamic women's movement was created. A new organization called the Women's Society of the Islamic Revolution was established soon after the Revolution.[124] The organization included members of highly educated women, many of whom held degrees from Europe or USA, who protested against the Shah. Although the organization adopted Islamic ideology, it did not get any support from the government. The conservatives thought that supporting such an organization might harm the new regime because, even though it encouraged the idea of the hejab, it warned the government to make it compulsory. Also, the organization was against abolishing the Family Protection Law.[125] As *Zan-e Ruz* was a widely available magazine for women, the hard-liners disapproved of its board editor and replaced her with one of their supporters. The organization

---

[123] Massoume Price. *A Brief History of Women's Movements in Iran 1850-2001.* [online] [undated] Available from:
http://www.parstimes.com/women/women_movements.html
[10th June. 2009]

[124] Haleh Afshar. *Islam and Feminisms An Iranian Case-Study.* (GB: Macmillan Press Ltd 2nd, 1999) pp 56,57.

[125] Hoodfar,H. (1999).

was very careful in presenting its idea of Islam ideology towards gender in order to avoid closure. In the same period, another Islamic wave appeared to raise both the idea of sex discrimination and how religion was used to benefit the patriarchal system.[126]

When the war with Iraq ended, the women's magazine raised the women's rights issue. In 1992, it discussed how Islam was misread to result in degrading women. On one hand, the feminist activists worked with human rights organizations but, on the other hand, they realized the importance of internationally acceptance by the government. As a result, the regime was prepared to discuss the gender issue more than any time since the revolution.[127] Faezeh Hashemi, Rafsanjani's daughter, was elected for the Fifth Majlis with the highest vote because she was one of the active feminists.[128] In the 1990s women regained some of rights they lost in the early days of the Revolution especially regarding the Family Law.[129] Also the government established the National Muslim Women's League in order to support all of women's organizations which now numbered over sixty.[130]

---

[126] Hoodfar,H. (1999).

[127] Hoodfar,H. (1999).

[128] Afshar, H. (1999) pp 56,57.

[129] Mahdi, A. (2004)

[130] Price,M.

When Khatami won the election in 1998, it was mainly because of his support of women's rights.[131] With regards to the Majlis, it was notable that the numbers of women candidates increased to 417 for the 2000 Majlis election. Some of elected women were liberal as well as other liberal male.[132]

The history of Iran has the most contradictory laws in the Middle East regarding women. Throughout the twentieth century, they experienced the most extreme forms of both fundamentalism and liberalism. While in the 1920s women were prohibited from wearing the veil, by the end of the 1970s they were not able to go in public without it. However, religion has played a major part in all of the three countries under consideration here. Since Qur'an could be interpreted in many different ways, many acts and laws could be described as 'Islamic' according to someone's beliefs. In all of the three ME countries, any kind of participation in the public sphere for women was denied, as women should not be seen or heard by strangers. If she does so, then it considered a disgrace for the family. Although the women in the early age of Islam were powerful participators politically and socially, and their memoirs are very well known and taught in all of the ME countries' schools,

---

[131]   Price,M.

[132]   Elham Gheytanchi. *Chronology of Events Regarding Women in Iran since the Revolution of 1979.*[online] [2000] Available from:
http://www.findrticles.com/p/articles/mi_m2267/is_2_67/ai_63787338
[Accessed 3rd July. 2009]

after several decades the opposite was true. Although Prophet Mohammad was proud of his wives and their manners later on and until now in some Arabic cultures, a husband would be very ashamed to say his wife's name in front of a stranger. Hundred years of the Ottmans' imperialism had its affect on traditions and beliefs, and some of these effects remain today.

5. THE WOMEN'S MOVEMENT IN THE UK

The women's movement issue in the UK means different campaigns for different issues concerning women. The earlier campaigns are called 'first-wave' feminism, and started early in the nineteenth century.[133] One of the main campaigns regarding women is the Women's Suffrage campaign which was launched in the mid nineteenth century. However, it is argued that the suffrage

---

[133]   Olive Banks. *Becoming a Feminist: The social origins of "first wave" feminism.* (Brighton: Wheatsheaf Books Ltd., 1986) pp 46.

campaign started when Mary Smith in 1832 handed a proposal to the Parliament when it was intended to amend the Reform Act to include more men voters.[134]

The Women's Suffrage movement started officially with the Langham Place meeting by a group of women in London in the 1850s. The meeting was led by Barbara Leigh, Smith Bodichon and Bessie Rayner Parkes. The group launched the English Women's Journal which specialised in the educational, political and employment rights for women. In his support for this movement, John Stuart Mill had included the women's rights in his election programme. Two suffrage societies then established one in London, and another in Manchester.[135]

While working on the suffrage campaign, a new Act was passed which inflamed women because of its double standard regarding sexuality. The Contagious Diseases Act that was passed in 1864 assumed that only women can spread the disease since it only subjected women to inspection.[136] At that time, there were

---

[134]   The National Archives. *The Campaign for the vote.* [online] [undated] Available from: http://www.learningcurve.gov.uk/britain1906to1918/g3/background.htm [Accessed 4th July. 2009]

[135]   Harold Smith. *The British Women's Suffrage Campaign 1866-1928.* (Essex: Addison Wesley Longman Limited, 1998) pp 3-14.

[136]   The purpose of this Act is to protect men in the British Army and Navy from having 'sexual diseases' that prostitutes might cause. The Act forced prostitutes to be examined, to prevent the spread of such disease.
Christie Zablocki . Contagious Diseases Act. [online] [undated] Available from: http://www.umd.umich.edu/casl/hum/eng/classes/434/charweb/zablocki3.htm [Accessed 4th July. 2009]

different suffrage societies for women in different cities. In 1867 the Manchester Society, led by Elizabeth Wolstenholme, united all of these societies into one group which was known as the National Society for Women's Suffrage (NSWS). A major argument of whether or not to support the Contagious Diseases campaign resulted in the withdrawal of the London Society from the National Society until 1877. Since owning a property was a condition to vote, and married women cannot own a property, this created another argument of whether or not to include married women. The London Society viewed that enfranchisement should be for single women; the Manchester Society included married women. The agreement between both societies was that the vote conditions that applied for men would be applied for women too, in case the property condition would change in the future.[137]

In spite of the argument that the word 'men' in Lord Brougham's Act includes both men and women unless it expressly excluded women, the idea was rejected by the Court of Common Pleas in 1868. In 1869, an important achievement for the suffragists was accomplished when Municipal Corporation Act allowed single women to vote.[138]

---

[137] Smith, H. (1998) pp 3-14. Also
Tanya Pohl. *Votes for Mothers*. [online] [2005] Available from:
http://dissertations.bc.edu/cgi/viewcontent.cgi?article=1098&context=ashonors
[Accessed 4th July. 2009]

[138] Philippa Levine. *Victorian Feminism 1850-1900*. (Essex: Anchor Brendon Ltd, 1997) pp 57-68.Also,Smith, (1998) pp 3-14.

Women's politics rights were introduced for the first time in Parliament in 1870.[139] It was introduced by the MP Jacob Bright who used to be an active member in the Manchester Society. When Mill was defeated in the 1868 election, Bright was the leader for women's politics rights in the Parliament. However, the bill did not pass mainly because the Prime Minister opposed it. The women's rights bill used to be introduced in every year during the 1870s. However, a disappointment occurred in 1884 when the suffrage for women did not pass when there were a general belief that it would. Although the vast majority of Liberals' supported the bill, the leaders were against it thinking that the majority of women would vote for the Conservative Party. On the contrary, the Conservatives leaders supported the women's right, but there were no intentions to introduce it because the majority of Conservatives MPs were opposed it. By the 1880s, there were two different attitudes concerning women. First, there were a group of women who opposed the suffrage rights for women. The anti-suffrages organised themselves in order to confront the suffrage campaign. Some of the men who opposed suffrage rights had supported the anti-suffrage group. Mary Ward was one of the main leaders who opposed the suffrage rights; she believed that the sexual attraction between men and women would prevent them from

---

[139] Manchester Central Library. *Women's Suffrage Cllection*. [online] [undated] Available from:
http://www.ampltd.co.uk/digital_guides/womens_suffrage_mcl_parts_1_and_2/Publishers-Note.aspx
[Accessed 2nd July. 2009]

working together in politics.[140] However, in 1918, the movement declared they had been beaten. On the other hand, the Corrupt Practice Act in 1883 was passed. The Act led to the dependence on voluntarily work during the election, banning paid agents. As most of the volunteers were women, the Liberal Party established the Women's Liberal Federation in 1887. Furthermore, women were allowed to be members in the Conservative Party's Primrose League to reach to 500 000 female members in 1891. In spite of the women's participation, the Primrose League of the Conservative Party did not allow the Party to be a women's rights lobby. When the Liberal Party's Women's group tried to pressurise the party to support women's suffrage, Gladstone, opposing women's suffrage, made a statement to the group to decide whether their loyalty was to the party or to the women's suffrage. Some of the women's party organizations had joined the NSWS, which resulted in the withdrawal of some of its member like Millicent Garret Fawcett and Lydia Becker to establish another organization called the Central Committee of the National Society for Women's Suffrage. The main aim of this organization was to avoid interference from the political parties since the NSWS did not allow any party to join before it changed its rule.[141] After 1890 working class women started joining the campaign when before it used to be composed

---

[140] Florence Boos. *The Campaign for Women's Suffrage 1865-1928(63 years)*. [online] [undated] Available from:
http://english.uiowa.edu/courses/boos/questions/womsuffrage.htm
[Accessed 2nd July. 2009] Also: Smith,H. (1998) pp 3-14.

[141] Jane Lewis. *Women and Social Action in Victorian and Edwardian England.* (Cheltenham: Edward Eglar, 1991) pp 240-250. Also, Smith,H. pp 3-14.

of the upper and middle class only. The North of England Society introduced a petition signed by more than twenty-nine thousand working women and given to the House of Commons in 1894. It was an important success for the women's movement when the Local Government Act allowed married women as well as single and widow to participate in the local election in 1894. In 1896 the suffrage societies merged into one union which was called the National Union of Women's Suffrage Societies (NUWSS). The union had one main purpose: to secure the suffrage rights for women.[142]

In 1907, the NUWSS planned a chain of protests. The first one was held in the same year in February. More than 3000 women participated representing forty women's organizations.[143]

In the beginning of the twentieth century, men's organizations for women's suffrage started to be formed. In London, the Men's League for Women's Suffrage was established in 1907, and others were established in Manchester and Scotland.[144] On the other hand, aware of the suffrage movement and its powerful development,

---

[142] Smith,H. pp 3-14. Also
National Union of Women's Suffrage Societies. *Records of the National Union of Women's Suffrage Societies.* [online] [undated] Available from:
http://www.aim25.ac.uk/cgi-bin/search2?coll_id=6639&inst_id=65
[Accessed 4th July. 2009]

[143] Smith,H. (1998) pp 3-14.

[144] John Rylands University Library collections. *Women's Suffrage Movement Archives.*[online] [undated] Available from:
http://rylibweb.man.ac.uk/data2/spcoll/mensuff/
[Accessed 5th July. 2009]

the anti-suffrage women established the Women's National Anti-Suffrage League in 1908.[145] The NUWSS succeeded to have as many members of women as possible from different social classes and different ethnic background by the start of the twentieth century.[146]

Another society called the Women's Social and Political Union (WSPU) was established in 1903 by Emmeline Pankhurst and her daughter Christable Pankhurst.[147] This union believed in using violence as the best way to secure suffrage rights for women. However, they did not want the violence to be life threatening. The organization used bombing and burning empty houses in order to prove their point.[148] Scores of them, both women and men, were imprisoned. They went on hunger-strike when they were not treated as political prisoners; the government ordered them to be force-fed. To prevent them from dying and becoming martyrs, the government published an act called the Temporary Discharge for Ill-Health which allowed the weak prisoners to be

---

[145]   In 1907, Sofia Londsdale was able to gather 37 000 signatures in a petition against the suffrage rights. The year after, the League was formed and signed a petition against such rights – the signatures numbered near to half million people (337, 018).
Janet S. Chafetz and Anthony G. Dworkin. In the Face of the Threat. *Gender and Society*. March 1987, 1 (1), pp 33-60.

[146]   Smith,H. (1998) pp 3-14.

[147]   Pohl, T. (2005).

[148]   Jenni Murray. *20th Century Britain: The Women's Hour*.[online] [1st Jan. 2001] Available from:
http://www.bbc.co.uk/history/british/modern/jmurray_01.shtml
[Accessed 5th July. 2009]

released, and when they regained their health, were rearrested again. Emily Davidson became the first martyr when she died from colliding with the King's horse in the Derby race. The NUWSS in Manchester supported the strategy of the WSPU at first, but then it believed that violence might be a drawback for the suffrage movement.[149] When the WW1 started in 1914, Christabel Pankhurst – the organization's leader - announced that the suffrage activities would be suspended.[150]

The NUWSS faced different tactics towards the war and had to choose from among them. Some argued that the organization should adapt the anti-war campaign and work with the peace movement. Others argued that they should support the government with the war decision. This argument was to defeat the opinion that women are pacifists and not trustworthy, so the organization might loose the support of some members of both Conservative and Labour Parties. Avoiding the split of the organization, it chose to follow the educational campaign; that is to publish articles about causes and prevention of war. Some of the women's suffrage organization continued with their activities for the campaign like Women's Freedom League. As the war continued, some of women's

---

[149] Welch,P. *Divisions in the women's suffrage movement.*[online] [June 2003] Available from:
http://pers-www.wlv.ac.uk/`le1810/suffdivs.htm
[Accessed 29th June. 2009]

[150] Susan Kent. *Making Peace: the reconstruction of gender in interwar Britain.* (New Jersey: Princeton University Press, 1993) pp 12-21. Also, Smith, H. (1998) pp 3-14.

societies had participated in demanding women's rights especially regarding the working issues.[151]

In 1916, the government intended to reform the election law in order to include the men in the armed forces.[152] That intention encouraged Fawcett to write a letter to the Prime Minister reminding him that any amendment to the election law should include women.[153] Moreover, Henderson and Cecil, who were ministers at that time, insisted that the amendment should include women or they would resign. This influential pressure meant that the government, especially the new Prime Minister Lloyd George, was more sympathetic with women's suffrage.[154]

As the issue of women's suffrage was very controversial between government members, the government held a Speaker's Conference. The conference issued a report giving women suffrage rights. Trying to limit the number of women elected so they would not form the majority, the report recommended two conditions:

1. Women should be either the occupier or the occupier's wife.

---

[151] Chery Law. *Suffrage and Power: the women's movement, 1918-1928.* (London: I.B. Tauris & Co Ltd., 1997) pp 13-23 Smith,H. (1998) pp 3-14.

[152] Laura Mayhall. Domesticating Emmeline: Representing the Suffragette, 1930-1993. *NWSA Journal.* 1999, 11 (2), pp 1-24.

[153] Susan Kent. The Politics of Sexual Differences. *Journal of British Studies.* July 1988, 27 (3), pp 232, 253.

[154] Smith,H. (1998) pp 3-14

2. The age limitation would be either 30 or 35.

The NUWSS was asked to accept the proposal or the government might drop the suffrage issue. However, the NUWSS demanded suffrage right for women with the same terms as men. The Organization voted to work on a campaign for alternative proposal. Also, different suffrage societies like the National Council for Adult Suffrage, the Independent Labour Party, and the Manchester and District Federation had rejected the proposal. Nevertheless, on March 1917, the Labour Party had approved the Speakers Report, while the Conservative Party was divided.[155]

The proposal was passed in House of Commons with a massive majority on 19 June 1917. It has been stated that the majority was an appreciation of women's role during the war. It specified that the women's age to be 30 or over, and added another condition that a woman should be local government elector or a wife of local government elector. In spite of the fact that the restrictions on women and discrimination against her which led to prevent many of them from voting, the women's societies had celebrated the Representation of the People Bill's and considerable achievement though it was not what they had demanded since the mid-19th century. Lady Astor was the first woman to enter the House of Commons as a MP in 1919.[156]

---

[155] Smith,H. (1998) pp 3-14.

[156] Pamela Horn. *Women in the 1920s.* (Gloucestershire: Alan Sutton Publishing Ltd., 1995) pp 1-24. Also Smith,H. (1998) pp 3-14.

After passing the suffrage Act, it was recognized that the restrictions meant that the majority of women remained voteless. As a result, the women's society started to reform to work for the new campaign demanding equal enfranchisement. Realizing the importance of the new voters,[157] the Conservative Party allowed women to be members, and organize a women's society right after passing the Act. Regardless of the fact that many MPs supported the equal enfranchisement, the equal suffrage right used to be presented each year during the 1920s, but it did not pass.[158]

Women became an important factor in elections, and can affect the victory for the political parties. By 1928, the women members in the Conservative party reached almost a million. Before the 1924 election one of the Conservative Party's leaders announced that the Party supported equal political rights for women. On the other hand, the NUWSS changed its name to the National Union of Societies for Equal Citizenship. Eleanor Rathbone became the first president.[159] The new organization announced that the equal franchise was not included in the Labour Party election programme. Moreover, some of the Labour Party's leaders announced they supported the equal franchise, but that they

---

[157] Rat Thane. *What Difference Did the Vote Make?*. [online] [undated] Available from: http://www.stm.unipi.it/Clioh/tabs/libri/2/05-Thane_53-82.pdf [Accessed 30th June. 2009]

[158] Smith,H. (1998) pp 3-14.

[159] Barbara Caine. *English Feminism 1780-1980*. (New York: Oxford University Press Inc., 1999) pp xvi.

should wait for the right time.[160]When the Conservative won the election, the debate was should the equal franchise be at the age of 21 or 25, noting that some of the politicians feared that women would form the majority of electoral.[161]

From the women's perspective, the Equal Political Rights Demonstration Committee arranged a demonstration supporting the equal franchise in 1926.[162] The rally was supported by forty women's organizations. As Rhondda announced that an action should be taken to pressure the government to pass the equal franchise, some were afraid of taking any militant action which would prevent any chances of getting the equal franchise.

The Cabinet formed a sub-committee in the purpose of the equal franchise issue; however, the sub-committee was terminated after three meetings due to a major argument regarding the age. Some members made the important argument that if they agreed on the age of 25, the next Labour government would change the age to 21 and gain the loyalty of women. By the end of the 1927, most of the Party Central Council members were in favour of the equal franchise in the age of 21.[163] For the second time the Bill was

---

[160]   Smith,H. (1998) pp 3-14.

[161]   Ibid.

[162]   Elizabeth Crawford. *The Women's Suffrage Movement: A Reference Guide 1866-1929*.(USA:Routledge, 2001) pp 513.

[163]   Law, C. (1997) pp 202-220,also Smith,H. (1998) pp 3-14.

passed in the House of the Commons with a massive majority in March 1928.[164]

By the end of the WW1, a new wave of feminists started to appear. Women like Maud Royden played a major part in the effort for men to admit that women are equal to them.[165] Eleanor Rathbone formed an organization in order to acknowledge women who did not gain the suffrage rights of their political rights in the Women's Citizens Association. Then, another association, called the Six Point Group, was formed by Rathbone from a number of women's organizations, to seek a woman's seat in the House of Lords.[166] During the 1930s,[167] feminists worked on legislating and amending legislations in order to embitter women's social position. It succeeded in several Acts such as the abolished of death penalty

---

[164] House of Commons Information Office. *Women in the House of Commons.* [online] [Oct. 2006] Available from:
http://www.parliament.uk/documents/upload/m04.pdf
[Accessed 13th July. 2009]

[165] Maud was a religious lady, her main focus is to prove that women are equal to men in general and in Church in specific.
The Women's Library. *The Paper of Agnes Muad Royden.*[online] [undated] Available from: http://www.archiveshub.ac.uk/news/0409amr.html
[Accessed 7th July. 2004]

[166] Kent, S.

[167] During the early 1930s - the period of the great depression - there were a large number of unemployed men. As such the attitude of the anti-feminist was to exclude women – especially married ones – from paid jobs.
Harold L. Smith. British Feminism and the Equal Pay Issue in the 1930s. *Ruotledge* (part of Taylor and Francis Group). March 1996, 5 (1), pp 97-110.

for mothers, the Divorce Act, the Inheritance Act, and Midwives Act.[168]

The women's movement had been affected by the WW2 impact. Although women's employment was raised highly in both paid and voluntary jobs, the trade unions, as well as the electrical and engineering unions which accepted women to be temporary members only, refused the apprenticeship right for women.[169] The war prepared the atmosphere for women's demands for equal pay. In 1943, the Equal Pay Campaign Committee (EPCC) was established.[170] The Women's Freedom League held a conference which was attended by about 20 women's organizations in order to harmonize women's activities. Then, the issue of equal pay became the main concern of the EPCC.[171]

For the purpose of women's rights, a new organization called Women for Westminster was established to encourage women to give their vote for women to be MPs.[172] The women's role was

---

[168]   Martin Pugh. *Women and the Women's Movement in Britain 1914-1999.* (London: Macmillan Press LTD, 2000) pp 236-244.

[169]   Pugh, M. (2000) pp 264-283.

[170]   Harold Smith. *Equal Pay and Opportunities.* [online] [undated] Available from: http://www.adam-matthew-publications.co.uk/digital_guides/sex_and_gender4/Editorial-Introduction.aspx
        [Accessed 7th July. 2009]

[171]   Pugh, M. (2000) pp 264-283. Also, for more details about the equal pay campaign: Harold Smith. The Problem of 'Equal Pay for Equal Work' in Great Britain During the WW2. *Journal of Modern History.* Dec. 1981, 53 (4), pp 652-672.

[172]   Amy Black and Stephen Brooke. The Labour Party, Women, and the Problem of Gender, 1951-1966. *Journal of British Studies.* Oct. 1997, 36 (4), pp 419-452.

been shifted after the war; while some remained in their jobs, many others return to their homes. Those who chose to continue working were shifted to more lowly jobs described as 'women's-job'. By the 1950s, equal pay was acceptable more than any other time. The fact that the 1950 election brought MPs from both major political parties almost equally; both parties wanted to use the equal pay issue for their own interest. Moreover, most of the MPs would vote in favour of the equal pay, and they did so in 1952 for Equal Pay for men and women teachers, and the equal pay for Civil Service. Although some trade unions established the Equal Pay Co-ordinating Committee, the equal pay in industry was avoided.[173]

During the 1960s a new slogan for the women's movement was raised which was the 'women's liberation'. It was not raised in the UK only, but it was slogan for feminists world wide.[174] There were several factors which motivated women's organizations to adapt the liberation move, including violence against women; lack of freedom, female opportunities in education; the achievement of equal pay; and so on. Many were optimistic for more modernisation when the new Labour government was elected in 1964. Harold Wilson, the Prime Minister, held his supporters' self-interests before women's issues. Regardless of some changes in legislations,

---

[173] Pugh, M. (2000) pp 285- 311.

[174] Vintee Sawhney. *The Women's Liberation Movement of the 1960s.* [online] [undated] Available from: http://www.cwluherstory.com/GrrlSmarts/sawhney.html [Accessed 4th July. 2009]

many had the impression that the 1960s government had the same standpoint towards women of the 1920s government. The first use of the 'women's liberation' expression was in 1967 when women were ignored in the New Left conferences. The liberation of the women movement were also affected by the highly participation of women in the peace movement which started in the 1950s. Four major demands for women were announced in the annually conference, which started in 1970 for that purpose:

1. Equal pay for equal work.
2. Equal opportunities and equal education.
3. Free contraception and abortion on demand.
4. Free 24 hour child care.[175]

The activists realized the importance of women's history: they started to make documentations about the history of the women's movement. Later on, by the 1990s, universities started to have courses on it and taught it as a subject called 'gender studies'. In addition, feminist presses started to form in order to be liberated from the media that were controlled by men, and which also accused women's activity of different allegations according to their personal interest. Although feminists worked under the same slogan 'women's liberation', there were three major approaches which had accordingly different starting point. There were the Radical, Social, and Liberal feminism. The need to protect

---

175 Tony Cliff. *Class Struggle and Women's liberation*. [online] [undated] Available from: http://www.marxists.org/archive/cliff/works/1984/women/11-wmvmtb.htm [Accessed 4th July.2009]

women from violence led to legislating the Domestic Violence and Matrimonial Proceedings Act in 1971. However, as that Act alone was not enough protection, a centre for rape crisis was established in London in 1976. A major protest was held in several cities against pornography which was blamed by feminists as being the main reason for violence and rape against women.[176]

After the success of legalising the contraceptive and the ability of women to obtain it from the NHS since 1963, regardless of their marital status, the movement raised the slogan 'A Women's Right to Choose' in support of the abortion. The campaign was organised by the National Abortion Campaign in 1975 despite the fact that abortion was allowed in 1967, albeit with some restrictions. Feminists were very active in this campaign by using different means such as the media, strikes, and gaining the support of the trade unions.[177]

In 1970 the Equal Pay Act was launched (amended in 1975) followed by the Sex Discrimination Act in 1975. Before legislating the Equal Pay Act, the Women's Liberation Movement held a conference demanding equal pay and equal opportunities. Moreover, an affective strike in Ford's Dagenham factory was made by women workers who demanded equal pay to men. Also, in 1964, the Working Women's Charter established and arranged

---

[176] Pugh, M. (2000) pp 312-333.

[177] Pugh, M. (2000) pp 312-333.

a proposal for the women workers' rights.[178] Due to some defaults in those two acts, both of them were amended. The Equal Pay Act was amended in 1983 and the Sex Discrimination Act was amended in 1986. Enquiries about equal pay and discrimination to the Equal Opportunity Commission reached 39,557 in 1993.[179]

By the late 1970s a different side of feminism started to demand greater sexual freedom. The view was that heterosexuality assured women's domination by men. Moreover, to these feminists, men were the enemies, so to achieve complete freedom for women they have to cut off any relationship with them.[180]

In the case of the news concerning the launch of cruise missiles containing nuclear warheads at Greenham Common in 1979, it was left to the peace movement to revitalise this motion. Most protests were organised spontaneously by women's organizations. They used the 'Women for Life on Earth' slogan, showing that male technological invention would destroy the earth. Although the peace campaign continued throughout the 1980s, the government

---

[178] Joni Lovenduski, Vicky Randall. *Contemporary Feminist Politics.* (New York: Oxford University Press, 1993) pp 179-182.

[179] Pamela Clayton. Social Citizenship and Political Rights of Women in the United Kingdom.[online] [April 1997] Available from: www.helsinki.fi/science/xantippa/wle/wle22.html [Accessed 7th July. 2009]

[180] Pugh, M. (2000) pp 312-333.

-- regardless of the fact that it was led by a woman as the prime minister -- did not change its policy towards nuclear weapons.[181]

In fact, the peace movement had started before that with the wide participation of women, two of whom became secretaries of the National Committee for the Abolition of Nuclear Weapon Tests. Also, a high number of women participated in a demonstration that walked from the Hyde Park to Trafalgar Square.[182]

As consequence of the women's liberation and the achievement of having different legislations in favour of women, violence against women continued. Despite the fact that the marriage rates were decreasing and divorce cases were rapidly increasing, women were the major victims of violence inside and outside marriage. Women Against Violence Against Women held a conference attended by 800 women in 1981. The most notable trends about women in the 1990s were the increase of single mothers; the postponement of bearing children in order to establish a career; and favouring cohabitation over marriage. Although in the 1990s women were accomplishing major successes in terms of education and employment, even though the number of professional women was rising, there still existed the 'glass ceiling' which prevented women

---

[181] Pugh, M. (2000) pp 334- 353.

[182] Elizabeth Wilson. *Only Halfway to Paradise.* (New York: Tavistock Publications, 1980) pp 177-180.

from being appointed to high level positions in spite of the launch of the 'Opportunity 2000' scheme.[183]

In addition to the maternity leave rights that were included in the Employment Rights Act in 1996, a remarkable legal change occurred in 1999 when the Maternity and Parental Leave Act was issued.[184] This new law gives the right to both mother and father to have leave for the sake of child care up to thirteen weeks. The Parental Leave Act equalises the chances of getting a job between men and women as now both sexes can leave for a period of time for parenting. Previously, employers preferred to appoint men as they would not leave work to take care of the child. Finally, the movement towards 'equality' was extended to include different kind of discriminations other than sex-based. The Race Relation Act, issued in 1976 and amended in 2000, prevents any discrimination that might be based on race, colour, nationality, or ethnic or national origin. If such discrimination took place in the workplace, training, education, housing, or in the services, the CRE (Commission for Racial Equality) is a non-governmental organisation responsible to put the Act into action.[185]

---

[183] Pugh, M. pp 334- 353.

[184] The Maternity and Parental Leave etc. Regulations 1999. [online] [1999] Available from:
www.legislation.hmso.gov.uk/si/si1999/19993312.htm
[Accessed 4th July.2009]

[185] Commission for Racial Equality (CRE). *The Race Relation Act.* [online] [undated] Available from:
www.cre.gov.uk/navigate/help.html
[Accessed 4th July.2009]

6. Conclusion

While there are a lot of similarities within the women's movement eras in the Middle Eastern countries, the movement in the UK is different especially when compared with Kuwait. The movement in the UK was well organized and focused on its main aim the suffrage rights. They believed in their cause and were willing to fight for it, as they did when the WSPU used violence as a way of pressure (for example, the day called 'Black Friday' as a result of one of their actions). Also, there were different societies in almost all over the UK. Furthermore, the suffrage societies had female as well as male members. Although there were men who opposed women's suffrage rights, there were many who supported that right for women and worked passionately for it. Moreover, regardless of the fact that some of the societies started with members from upper and middle classes, later on they succeeded in having members that represented all of the society's classes. The two main political parties used the issue as a tactic knowing the right time of using it. Sometimes, some of the party members believed in suffrage rights for women, but rather to be more loyal to the majority of the party members who were opposed to it.

On the other hand, before the oil discovery in Kuwait, there is no record of any women's movement. Due to the fact they were secluded, and could not go out, they did not socialise with other women unless they were relatives or neighbours. Although in other neighbouring countries women participated in some activities even in politics, there was not any participation in the public sphere in Kuwait. That could reflect the cruelty and the absolute domination of women.

When the women's movement started in Kuwait, it was for the purpose of modernizing women. The demand for the suffrage rights did not start until a decade after establishing the women's organizations. The resolve of AWDS affected the political movement for women, because the WSCC did not start campaigning for women's political rights until later in the 1980s. The effort for the women's rights was not well organized, and it is excluded for the members from the upper-class women. Some modest demonstrations were made on every Election Day every four years, attended by a few women. No organization had been established for the purpose of the women's political rights issue. Although when there are some MPs who supported women's rights, the opposition movement was always stronger. Even when the Amir issued the decree of women's rights in 1999, it did not pass in the Parliament.

Whereas there was a minority of people who were against the suffrage right for women in the UK, they are in the majority in Kuwait and are supported by some Islamists. In a study done by the AWDS in 1970, 51% of women were against the suffrage rights for women.[186]

On the other side of the argument, there are a lot of similarities in the movements between the ME countries. In all of them, veiling was a main obstacle to their freedom although Iran and Egypt struggled more over it. Women in all of the three countries considered here were denied their rights even after the participation in a major national event whether it was war, revolution, or occupation.

A major fact that differentiates between the three ME countries and the UK, other than culture and tradition, is religion which is arguably the reason for the creation of traditions and cultures. In Muslim countries people live according to different traditions and beliefs. In Kuwait, where 99% of the people are Muslims, there

---

[186] Al-Sadani, N. pp 97.

are great differences between the Bedouins and the city dwellers. Regardless of the fact that Bedouins do not live in the desert any more, and they live in the city, they still have a different culture from the city dwellers. Female Bedouins still get married without giving their consent or even seeing their future husband before marriage; many of them are forced to wear the veil, and can only be educated in an all-female college instead of the co-educational. If she gets married while still student, then her husband has the full authority to decide whether she should continue her studies or not. Many of these women are not permitted to drive or to own a car as it is considered 'shameful'. None of the above is the case for the town people.

As stated before, when the enfranchisement for the women's bill failed more than once in parliament, the Islamists were unable to come up with reasons based on Islam, whether from Qur'an or Hadith. It is noteworthy that most of the MPs then, were Islamists and most of those Islamists are Bedouins. Therefore, this mix between traditions and religion made it difficult for the draft to be passed if it was not for the political pressures from inside or, mainly, outside Kuwait. The coalition that liberated Kuwait enforced more of its democratic acts, and the women's right is one of these.[187], This is especially so since three Gulf countries, Oman, Bahrain, and Qatar, recently established a parliament and voting

---

[187]   Ferry Biedermann. *The Struggle for Women's Rights in Kuwait.* [online] [26th April 2001] Available from:
www2.rnw.nl/rnw/en/currentaffairs/region/middleeast/kuwait.html
[Accessed 4th July. 2009]

as a new system to accomplish democracy, and women took part in it alongside men.

As women's rights are seen to be more of a political issue in the other countries that was studied in this book, it is also true in the case of Kuwait. The Islamists had to change their oppositional position to supporting it in order to gain more votes. It is true when knowing that in 2006 election which it was the first election that women participated in, they voted for previous MPs who were against giving women the political rights.

BIBLIOGRAPHY

Books

Ahmad Taha. *Almara' Kefahoha wa Amaloha* (Woman: their Strugele and Hope). (Cairo: Dar Al-Jmaheer, 1964)

Aida Beshara. *The Role of Women in Integrated Development in Egypt.*(London: State University of New York Press, 1987)

Amal Al-Sabki. *Alharaka Alnesae'ya fe Maser* (Women's Movement in Egypt).(Eygpt: Al-Haya' Al-Mesreya Al-Amman Lel-Ketab, 1986)

Amani Saleh. *Women in Modern Culture and Society: A Century of Arabic Discourse*. (Demascus: Dar Al-Fik, 2002)

Asghar Fathi. *Women and the Family in Iran*. (Netherlands: E.J. Brill, 1985)

Baqer Al-Najar, *AlMara' fe Alkhalej Alarabi wa Tahawelat Alhadatha Alaseera* (Women In the Arabian Peninsula). (Beirut: Al-Markaz Al-Thagafe Al-Arabi, 2000) pp 15-30.

Barbara Caine. *English Feminism 1780-1980*. (New York: Oxford University Press Inc., 1999)

Beth Baron. *The Women's Awakening in Egypt*.(New York: Yale University, 1994)

Camron Amin. *The Making of the Modern Iranian Women*. (Florida: University Press of Florida, 2002)

Chery Law. *Suffrage and Power: the women's movement, 1918-1928*. (London: I.B. Tauris & Co Ltd., 1997)

Elizabeth Wilson. *Only Halfway to Paradise*. (New York: Tavistock Publications, 1980)

Eliz Sanasarian. *The Women's Rights Movement in Iran*. (New York: praege Publishers, 1982)

Farah Azari. *Women of Iran*. (London: Ithaca Press London, 1983)

Haleh Afshar. *Islam and Feminisms An Iranian Case-Study.* (GB: Macmillan Press Ltd 2nd, 1999)

Haleh Esfandiari. *Reconstructed Lives.* (Washington DC: The Woodrow Wilson Centre Press,1997)

Harold Smith. *The British Women's Suffrage Campaign 1866-1928.* (Essex: Addison Wesley Longman Limited, 1998)

Haya Al-Mughni, *Women in Kuwait The Politics of Gender.* (London: Saqi Books,2001)

Huda Sha'rawi. *Auto-biography of Huda Sha'rawi.* (Syria: Al-Mada House, 2003)

Joni Lovenduski, Vicky Randall. *Contemporary Feminist Politics.* (New York: Oxford University Press, 1993)

Laila Abu-Lughod. *Remaking Women.* (Princeton, N.J.: Princeton University Press, 1998)

Latefa Salem. *Al-Mara' Al-Masreya wa Al-Tagyer Al-Ejtemae' 1919-1945* Egyptian Women and Social Changes 1919-1945). (Cairo: Al-Haya' Al-Masreya Al-Amma lelketab, 1984) pp

Leila Ahmad. Early Feminism Movements in The ME. In: *Muslim Women.* (Australia: Croom Helm Australia Pty Ltd., 1984)

Majda S. Makhlouf. *Al-Harem fe Al-Ghasr Al-Othmani* (The Harem in the Othman Palace). (Cairo: Dar Al-Afagh Al-Arabeyia, 1998)

Majed Badran. *Ahwal Alnesa' fe Masr* (Women's Conditions in Egypt). (Cairo: Dar Aldewan,1996)

Margret Badran. Kuwaiti Women in the Batlle: Before and After the Iraqi Occupation. In: *Islam, Gender and Social Changes.* (Amman: Al-Ahleyia, 2003)

Martin Pugh. *Women and the Women's Movement in Britain 1914-1999.* (London: Macmillan Press LTD, 2000)

Nadje Al-Ali. *Secularism, Gender and the State in the Middle East.* (Cambridge: University Press, 2000)

Nouria Al-Sadani. *Alharakat Alnesae'ya fe Algharn Aleshreen 1917-1981* (The Arabic Women's Movement in the 20th Century). (Kuwait, 1982)

Nouria Al-Sadani, *Almasera Altarekheya Lelheghogh Alseyaseya Lelmara' Alkwaytia* (History of Kuwaiti Women Suffrage Rights Movement). (Kuwait: Dar Al-Syasa, 1983)

Olive Banks. *Becoming a Feminist: The social origins of "first wave" feminism.* (Brighton: Wheatsheaf Books Ltd., 1986)

Pamela Horn. *Women in the 1920s.* (Gloucestershire: Alan Sutton Publishing Ltd., 1995)

Parvin Paidar. *Women and the political process in the twentieth-century Iran.* (New York: Cambridge University Press, 1995)

Philippa Levine. *Victorian Feminism 1850-1900.* (Essex: Anchor Brendon Ltd, 1997)

Jane Lewis. *Women and Social Action in Victorian and Edwardian England.*(Cheltenham: Edward Eglar, 1991)

Ruth F. Woodsmall. *Moslem Women Enter A New World.* (NY: AMS Press, 1975)

Sa'ad A. Al-Haji. *Al-Jame'yat Al-Nesae'ya Al-Ejtemae'ya* (Women's Cultural Societies).(1983 Sa'ad A. Al-Haji. *Al-Jame'yat Al-Nesae'ya Al-Ejtemae'ya* (Women's Cultural Societies).(1983

Sabeeka M. Al-Najar. Al-Haraka Al-Nesae'ya fe Al-Khaleej (Women's Movemen in the Gulf) In: Violet Dagher. *Al-Mara' wa Al-Osra fe Al-Mojtama't Al-Khaleejeya (Women and Family in the Gulf Societies).* (France: Editions Eurabe, 2004)

Soha Abdel-Kader. *Egyptian Women in Changing Society, 1899-1987.* (Colorado: Lynne Rienner Publishers,Inc,1987)

Susan Kent. *Making Peace: the reconstruction of gender in interwar Britain.* (New Jersey: Princeton University Press, 1993)

Working and Conference Papers

Mohammad Al-Rumaihi. Athar Alnaft ala Wathe' Almara' Alarabia fe Alkhaleej. In: Al-Mara' wa Douroha fe Harakat Al-Wehda Al-Arabia (Women's Role in Arab Unity). Ali Shalaq 'et. al'. (Lebanon: Markaz Derasat Al-Wehda Al-Arabia, 1993) pp 231-251.

Articles

Ali A. Mahdi. The Iranian Women's Movement: A Century Long Struggle. *The Muslim World*. Oct. 2004, 94 (4), pp 427-448.

Amy Black and Stephen Brooke. The Labour Party, Women, and the Problem of Gender, 1951-1966. *Journal of British Studies*. Oct. 1997, 36 (4), pp 419-452.

Azar Tabari. The Women's Movement in Iran: A Hopeful Prognosis. *Feminist Studies*. 1986, 12 (2), pp 342-360.

Harold L. Smith. British Feminism and the Equal Pay Issue in the 1930s. *Ruotledge* (part of Taylor and Francis Group). March 1996, 5 (1), pp 97-110.

Harold Smith. The Problem of 'Equal Pay for Equal Work' in Great Britain During the WW2. *Journal of Modern History*. Dec. 1981, 53 (4), pp 652-672.

Janet S. Chafetz and Anthony G. Dworkin. In the Face of the Threat. *Gender and Society.* March 1987, 1 (1), pp 33-60.

Laura Mayhall. Domesticating Emmeline: Representing the Suffragette, 1930-1993. *NWSA Journal.* 1999, 11 (2), pp 1-24.

Moghadam. Revolution, the State, Islam, and Women. *Social Text.* 1989, 22, pp 40-61.

Susan Kent. The Politics of Sexual Differences. *Journal of British Studies.* July 1988, 27 (3), pp 232, 253.

WebPages and published documents

Abdul-Kareem Sulaiman. *Al-Islameyon wa Al-Mara'* (Woman and the Islamists).[online] [2nd July.2004] Available from:
http://www.rezgar.com/debat/show.art.asp?aid=20159
[Accessed 14th June.2009]

Al-Talea. *Annervarsy of the Human Rights Scociety.* [online] [29th June. 2005] Available from:
http://www.taleea.com/newsdetails.php?id=4854&ISSUENO=1684
[Accessed 4th Nov. 2006]

Arab News. *Birth of Ahmad Orabi (A Revolutionary Leader).*[online] [31st Mar.2001] Available from:
http://www.arabicnews.com/ansub/Daily/Day/010331/2001033136.html
[Accessed 28 th May.2009]

Ayad Al-Qazzat. *Education of Women in the Arab World.* [online] [undated] Available from: http://www.library.cornell.edu/colldev/mideast/awomeduc.htm [Accessed 14th June. 2009]

CNN. *Kuwaiti liberals propose women's rights bill, again.* [online] [29th July 2000] Available from: http://archives.cnn.com/2000/WORLD/meast/07/29/kuwait.women.rights.ap/index.html [Accessed 2nd May.2009]

Christie Zablocki . Contagious Diseases Act. [online] [undated] Available from: http://www.umd.umich.edu/casl/hum/eng/classes/434/charweb/zablocki3.htm [Accessed 4th July. 2009]

Dewan Al-Arab. *Nouria Al-Sadani.* [online] [29th July 2006] Available from: http://www.diwanalarab.com/spip.php?article5356&vo=56 [Accessed 1st May.2009]

Dr. Zayar. *The Iranian Revolution- Past, Present and Future.* [online] [undated] Available from: http://www.marxist.com/the-iranian-revolution-past-present-future.htm [Accessed 12th June.2009]

Elham Gheytanchi. *Chronology of Events Regarding Women in Iran since the Revolution of 1979.*[online] [2000] Available from:

http://findarticles.com/p/articles/mi_m2267/is_2_67/ai_63787338/
[Accessed 3rd July. 2009]

Fat'hi Aamer. *Qasim Amin fe Mahakim Al-taftesh* (Qasim Amin in Inquisitions).[online] [19th Dec.2004] Available from: http://www.al-araby.com/articles/939/041219-939-pnp01.htm
[Accessed 7th Feb.2006]

Feminist Majority Foundation. *Kuwait.* [online] [5th July 2000] Available from: http://www.feminist.org/news/newsbyte/news_results.asp?us=1&glo.
[Accessed 7th Feb.2009]

Ferry Biedermann. *The Struggle for Women's Rights in Kuwait.* [online] [26th April 2001] Available from: http://www.rnw.nl/hotpots/html/kuwait01426.html.
[Accessed 2nd April.2009]

Homa Hoodfar. *The Women's Movement in Iran.* [online] [1999] Available from: http://www.iranchamber.com/society/articles/women_secularization_islamization1.php
[Accessed 3rd June. 2009]

Jouslin H. Al-Debs. *Huda Sha'rawi.* [online] [6th Mar.2004] Available from: http://www.daralhayat.com/society/03-2004/20040305-06p18-01.txt/story.html

[Accessed 8th Nov. 2004]

Kareema Hasan. *Rae'dat Sahafeyat mn Zamin Fat* (Journalists Women in the Passed Decades). [online] [14th April.2006] Available from:
http://harakamasria.org/node/5719
[Accessed 8th March.2009].

Mahrajan Al-Qurain Al-Thaghafi (the Eleventh) Al-Quarain Cultural Festival. [online] [Dec.2004] Available from:
http://www.kuwaitculture.org/alqurain2004/taghderia.htm#book3-1
[Accessed 4th April. 2009]

Mamdoh Esmae'l. *Al-Hejab wa Ma'rakat Al-Tagreeb* (The Veil and the Battle of Westernization). [online] [16th Jan.2004] Available from:
http://al-shaab.org/GIF/16-01-2004/c1.htm
[Accessed 8th June.2009]

Mark, Arya and Robin. *Anarki in Iran.* [online] [19th Sep.2005] Available from:
http://www.kefaya.org/05znet/051005baymenbidar.htm
[Accessed 10th June.2009]

Massoume Price. *A Brief History of Women's Movements in Iran 1850-2001.*[online] [undated] Available from:
http://www.parstimes.com/women/women_movements.html
[Accessed10th June. 2009]

Mehrangiz Kar. *The Legal Status of Iranian Women.*[online] [18th April 2000] Available from:
http://www.iranian.com/Opinion/2000/April/Women/
[Accessed 17th June.2009]

Mohammad Emara (Islam online website). *Qasim Amin.* [online] [undated] Available from:
http://www.islamonline.net/Arabic/history/1422/06/article19a.shtml
[Accessed 7th Feb.2009].

Mohammad Mansour. *Ba'd Najaheha Fe Ghadeyat Al-Mara' Al-Kuwaitia* (After The Success of Passing the Women's Suffrage Rights). [online] [2006] Available from:
http://www.ahl-alquran.com/arabic/show_article.php?main_id=373
[Accessed 4th Nov. 2008]

Muddafar Abdulla. *Interview with Dr.Seham Al-Fraih.* [online] [3rd Aug.2005] Available from:
http://www.taleea.com/newsdetails.php?id=5214&ISSUENO=1689
[Accessed 8th Nov. 2006]

Nabeela Hashim. *Aisha Al-Taimouriya.* [online] [undated] Available from:
http://cmadp.com/taymur.htm
[Accessed 8th Nov.2004]

Nikki R. Keddie. *Women in Iran Since 1979.* [online] [2000] Available from:
http://www.iranchamber.com/society/articles/women_iran_since_1979.php
[Accessed 10th June. 2009]

Pedram Missaghi. *First protests against mandatory hijab.*[online] [7th March 2000] Available from:
http://www.iranian.com/History/2000/March/Women/index.html
[Accessed 17th June.2009]

The Institute for compilation and Publication of Imam Khomeini's Work. *The Position of Women From the Viewpoint of Imam Khomeini.* [online] [2001] Available from:
http://www.iranchamber.com/history/rkhomeini/books/women_position_khomeini.pdf
[Accessed 20th June.2009].

The Library of Congress. *Kuwait- Society.* [online] [undated] available from:
http://www.country-data.com/cgi-bin/query/r-7583.html
[Accessed 11th June. 2009]

The National Archives. *The Campaign for the vote.* [online] [undated] Available from:
http://www.learningcurve.gov.uk/britain1906to1918/g3/background.htm
[Accessed 4th July. 2009]

The New York Times. *Kuwait Rejects Political Rights for Women.*
[online] [24th Nov.1999]Available from: http://chora.virtualave.
net/kuwaitrejectswomen.htm
[Accessed 2nd March.2009]

The Official Website of the State of Kuwait. *Al-Ta'leem fe Al-
Kuwait Ghabl Ekteshaf Al-Naft (Education in Kuwait Before Oil
Discovery).* [online] [undated] Available from:
http://www.kuwait.kw/Diwan/main/Story_Of_Kuwait/Kuwait_
before_Oil/Social_Life/education.html#WomanEdu11
[Accessed 5th Nov. 2004]

Ulil Abdulla. *Islam, Women, and Heresy.* [online] [24th Oct.2003]
Available from:
http://www.umich-cseas.org/eventsandnews/abstracts/ULIL/
Third%20talk.htm
[Accessed 8th June.2009]

Women Literature Assosation of UAE. *Dureya Shafeq.*[online]
[26th Oct.2004] Available from:
http://www.alrabetta.ae/Read2247.html
[Accessed 14th June.2009]

Tanya Pohl. *Votes for Mothers.* [online] [2005] Available from:
http://dcollections.bc.edu/R/XQMRXQCIQM593UC92HFKG
8A7REV3KF47LX7LF328PSEJMRPPU5-00585?func=results-
jump-full&set_entry=000007
[Accessed 4th July. 2009]

Manchester Central Library. *Women's Suffrage Cllection.* [online] [undated] Available from: http://www.ampltd.co.uk/digital_guides/womens_suffrage_mcl_parts_1_and_2/Publishers-Note.aspx [Accessed 2nd July. 2009]

Florence Boos. *The Campaign for Women's Suffrage 1865-1928(63 years).* [online] [undated] Available from: http://english.uiowa.edu/courses/boos/questions/womsuffrage.htm [Accessed 2nd July. 2009]

National Union of Women's Suffrage Societies. *Records of the National Union of Women's Suffrage Societies.* [online] [undated] Available from: http://www.archiveshub.ac.uk/news/0712nuwss.html [Accessed 4th July. 2009]

John Rylands University Library collections. *Women's Suffrage Movement Archives.*[online] [undated] Available from: http://rylibweb.man.ac.uk/specialcollections/collections/guide/atoz/womenssuffrage/ [Accessed 5th July. 2009]

Jenni Murray. *20th Century Britain: The Women's Hour.*[online] [1st Jan. 2001] Available from: http://www.bbc.co.uk/history/british/modern/jmurray_01.shtml [Accessed 5th July. 2009]

Penny Welch. *Divisions in the women's suffrage movement.*[online] [June 2003] Available from: http://pers-www.wlv.ac.uk/~le1810/suffdivs.htm [Accessed 29th June. 2009]

Rat Thane. *What Difference Did the Vote Make?.* [online] [undated] Available from: http://www.stm.unipi.it/Clioh/tabs/libri/2/05-Thane_53-82.pdf [Accessed 30th June. 2009]

House of Commons Information Office. *Women in the House of Commons.* [online] [Oct. 2006] Available from: http://www.parliament.uk/documents/upload/m04.pdf [Accessed 13th July. 2009]

The Women's Library. *The Paper of Agnes Muad Royden.*[online] [undated] Available from: http://www.archiveshub.ac.uk/news/0409amr.html [Accessed 7th July. 2009]

Harold Smith. *Equal Pay and Opportunities.* [online] [undated] Available from: http://www.adam-matthcw-publications.co.uk/digital_guides/ sex_and_gender4/Editorial-Introduction.aspx [Accessed 7th July. 2009]

Vintee Sawhney. *The Women's Liberation Movement of the 1960s.* [online] [undated] Available from: http://www.uic.edu/orgs/cwluherstory/_notes/GrrlSmarts/ sawhney.html

[Accessed 4th July. 2009]

Tony Cliff. *Class Struggle and Women's liberation.* [online] [undated] Available from:
http://www.marxists.org/archive/cliff/works/1984/women/11-wmvmtb.htm
[Accessed 4th July.2009]

Pamela Clayton. Social Citizenship and Political Rights of Women in the United Kingdom.[online] [April 1997] Available from:
www.helsinki.fi/science/xantippa/wle/wle22.html
[Accessed 7th July. 2009]

The Maternity and Parental Leave etc. Regulations 1999. [online] [1999] Available from:
www.legislation.hmso.gov.uk/si/si1999/19993312.htm
[Accessed 4th July.2009]

Commission for Racial Equality (CRE). *The Race Relation Act.* [online] [undated] Available from:
http://www.opsi.gov.uk/si/si2003/20031626.htm
[Accessed 4th July.2009]

Ferry Biedermann. *The Struggle for Women's Rights in Kuwait.* [online] [26th April 2001] Available from:
http://static.rnw.nl/migratie/www.radionetherlands.nl/currentaffairs/region/middleeast/kuwait010426.html-redirected
[Accessed 4th July.2009]

www.ingramcontent.com/pod-product-compliance
Lightning Source LLC
Chambersburg PA
CBHW030349290526
45785CB00004B/1663